Don't Let It Get You Down

Essays on Race, Gender, and the Body

Savala Nolan

SIMON & SCHUSTER

New York   London   Toronto   Sydney   New Delhi

Simon & Schuster
1230 Avenue of the Americas
New York, NY 10020

Names and identifying characteristics of some individuals have been changed.

Previous versions of *Dear White Sister* and *Fat in Ways White Girls Don't Understand* ran in Bust.com.

Excerpts from SHADES OF BLACK by Sandra L. Pinkney. Text copyright © 2000 by Sandra L. Pinkney. Reprinted by permission of Scholastic Inc.

First Simon & Schuster hardcover edition July 2021

SIMON & SCHUSTER and colophon are trademarks of Simon & Schuster, Inc.

For information about special discounts for bulk purchases, please contact Simon & Schuster Special Sales at 1-866-506-1949 or business@simonandschuster.com.

The Simon & Schuster Speakers Bureau can bring authors to your live event. For more information or to book an event, contact the Simon & Schuster Speakers Bureau at 1-866-248-3049 or visit our website at www.simonspeakers.com.

Interior design by Carly Loman

Manufactured in the United States of America

10 9 8 7 6 5 4 3 2 1

Library of Congress Cataloging-in-Publication Data

Names: Trepczynski, Savala N., author.
Title: Don't let it get you down : essays on race, gender, and the body / Savala N. Trepczynski.
Description: New York, NY : Simon & Schuster, [2021]
Identifiers: LCCN 2020046649 | ISBN 9781982137267 (hardback) | ISBN 9781982137281 (trade paperback) | ISBN 9781982137298 (ebook)
Subjects: LCSH: Feminine beauty (Aesthetics)—United States. | Body image—United States. | Feminism—United States. | Interracial dating—United States. | Racially mixed people—United States.
Classification: LCC HQ1220.U5 T64 2021 | DDC 305.420973—dc23
LC record available at https://lccn.loc.gov/2020046649

ISBN 978-1-9821-3726-7
ISBN 978-1-9821-3729-8 (ebook)

For Mom

For Dad

Contents

Introduction

In 1997, at the age of sixteen, I left my home in California to spend the summer in New York City. I stayed in the luxurious apartments of the prep school kids I'd befriended that spring at the Mountain School, an idyllic, warmhearted, working farm in Vermont where we'd all participated in an elite semester-long program for high school juniors. I wore size 26 pants—that's a women's plus-size 26—sported worn-out cornrows and acne, and had divorced parents and no money. Except for my mind—which got me into an exclusive program like the Mountain School—I was nothing like the Manhattan teenagers who hosted me, who lived in apartments with staff entrances and Picassos hung casually in hallways, who carried twenty-dollar lip balm and had faces as clear and cared-for as pearls, who were both profligate and cheap in the unusual way of the wealthy, thinking nothing of three-hundred-dollar dinners yet walking an extra four blocks to buy the cheapest pack of cigarettes.

I think our friendships were real. I think they loved me, and it was mutual. But I can never know how much of their love was tethered to the sheer delight and surprise of meeting a fat brown girl on scholarship who could quote Wordsworth, whose family came to America in the 1600s, who wore preppy clothes, even if big. Whether our friendships were deeply honest or a little bit rotten, when we hung out I always felt I was listening—eavesdropping—from another room, ear pressed to the wall. They were tip-top upper class; I was with them, but not of them. I heard what they said and, like a spy, observed how they moved, their words and actions rich with layers of meaning even they didn't understand because fish never fully understand the water. That summer's experience, when I felt my incredible proximity to power but also my irreconcilable distance from it, has stayed with me. It has, in fact, been one of the defining dynamics of my life.

I call myself in-between: I'm a mixed Black woman and what folks have sometimes called "a whole lot of yellow wasted," meaning I have light (yellow) skin "wasted" by Black features (kinky hair, broad nose). I'm Mexican on my dad's side, but I don't speak Spanish. I'm descended from enslaved people on my dad's side, but slaveholders on my mom's side. Their progeny disowned her and her future kids when she married a Black man. I'm a Daughter of the American Revolution. My mom completed graduate school, as did I; my dad didn't finish elementary school and spent nearly twenty years incarcerated (a few years here, a few years there). I started my first diet at age three or four, and have been painfully thin and truly fat, multiple times, for thirty years, which is to say I know things about womanhood that you can't know if your body is normal or your weight hasn't fluctuated wildly. I'm a lawyer, and in law school I worked for the United States Attorney's Office and the Obama administration, and as a child I watched my dad deal cocaine to pay child support. I went to tony private schools and grew up in Marin County, which had the world's highest per capita income in those days; I also sometimes spent weekends with my dad, who was so poor we went to the bathroom in buckets under a ceiling hole repaired with a tarp.

This book began as a way to process my own dislocation, as the kind of cartography we all do to address certain ambiguities in our lives. Ultimately, it is about living between society's most charged, politicized, and intractably polar spaces: between Black and white, between rich and poor, between thin and fat (as a woman). It's about the processes of growing up, dating, working, mothering, and self-discovering while occupying these interstitial identities. I live on the balcony and the dance floor at the same time, and my story is rooted in my body: a brown, female, and currently fat body the world more or less despises, and onto which the culture ascribes a bizarre constellation of faults, sins, fates, and histories; and also a body with light-skin privilege, and access to thin privilege, and which has successfully carried me through elite spaces from the White House to Park Avenue apartments. Through the eyes of my body, I see the world's dominant cultures and subordinated cultures as an insider and an outsider at once. I wrote this book to illuminate these dominant and subordinated spaces, and the space that both separates and binds them. I wrote it to articulate a space in between.

On Dating White Guys
While Me

Holt was a catch and I thought maybe we were heading somewhere, but then I saw his feet, and they were beautiful, unlike
mine. Dating requires intimacy: bare feet, side by side, maybe
touching at the foot of a bed, in the sand, the grass. I did not
want to place my feet next to his.

His feet were smooth and well-shaped as if carved from
marble, with neat cuticles and nails filed symmetrically. When
I saw them I thought, *They're like* David's *right foot!* Years before, I'd sketched *David*'s feet in charcoal, full of hope, the
filtered light as gentle as a powder puff in the Florentine museum, a hushed flow of tourists and art students around me. I
wish I'd sketched the slaves and their pocked granite confines
instead, but back then, in the spring of 2002, it was *David* who
spoke to me. He was being cleaned with water and Q-tips,
by erudite Italians kneeling on scaffolding beside his pensive
brow; that's how Holt's feet seemed to me—like things another person would carefully clean for him.

There were many things about Holt that I liked. I liked how

his biceps emerged from T-shirt sleeves. I liked how he stood next to me at that Christmas party on Benvenue Ave., brushed up and emitting a gently possessive warmth that made me giddy. I liked getting breakfast with him early in the morning at the coffee shop that served so-so coffee, and I liked how it looked to anyone walking by: me, with him. I liked how he lingered when I drove him home that brisk autumn night, leaning back into the car, suggesting we get together soon to study—we were in law school—his big-nosed face and impish smile illuminated by porchlight. I liked that he was from New York, that he was smart, that his dad was an iffy presence in his life, like mine. That his sneakers were always clean, that he drank gobs of whiskey and beer and never seemed drunk, that his East Coast self-possession shone brightly against the floppy California exuberance in which we lived.

And I liked that he was white. I liked his whiteness in an uncomfortable, subterranean way. I'd long sensed that the most succinct, irrefutable way to move up in the world was to be loved by a prototypical white man—i.e., someone at the top. There's a cultural magic in their approval, a kind of magnetizing glitter that surrounds the approved-of object. So, I pursued them. I had relationships with men of color, too; but a certain type of white guy had a particular hold on my psyche. I hoped, in landing one, to earn a medal. To sling it around my neck and prove that I wasn't too low on the ladder for blessings. Adjacent to them, accepted by them, I'd undo the injuries of not belonging I'd endured. I'd become the girl I'd ached and tried my whole childhood and adolescence to be: a version of that fairylike, Nordic blonde in a Timotei shampoo commercial, over whom I obsessed as a child, floating on my back in the bath and imagining my brown, cotton-candy hair was a white silk ribbon, like hers.

Holt had potential. He could be my world of oysters. We clicked; he seemed to see that I was bright, credentialed, special. He, with his jocular, confident whiteness, could slay my otherness, rescue me from the ogre of myself. I'd grieve, yes, but then watch my life bloom, unfettered by bigness, by brownness. I really believed this—until I saw his feet, which were so handsome—sophisticated, even—compared to mine.

I saw them on a cool November night. We were in his kitchen drinking Two Buck Chuck as he fried salmon burgers and his roommates watched television. His long torso in a white T-shirt was so satisfying there, spatula in hand, rough whoosh of thick, sandy-blond hair on his head and gum-droppy lips saying something or other, basketball shorts low on his hips, when I looked down—how had I never seen them before?—to his feet on the terra-cotta kitchen tile. They were *lovely*. I almost blurted it out. Fizzy heat needled up my spine and sloshed down the front of my head as I thought how my own feet, shoved suddenly deeper into my shoes, were a particular kind of not beautiful, a *big* that attached to and amplified my blackness, my poorness, my body-bigness.

Laila Ali says she gets pedicures because her feet are a women's size twelve and (she laughs) nobody wants to see them big old thangs looking more mannish than they already do. Her words, uttered in a husky voice with a toss of her straightened hair, have memed in my head for years. There's no hiding big feet (like hers, mine are twelves or thirteens), even in hyperfeminine ballet flats, or carefree Havaianas, or high heels. And my feet are often dry because I never apply the shea butter I buy. And I rarely get pedicures because they're expensive and exploitative and don't actually change the size and shape of your feet.

My feet have always struck me as my tell of otherness, even more than my nose, or hair, or weight. No matter the private schools, the white-sounding voice, the white-sounding name, or how I put white people at ease, especially rich white people, my feet seemed to cast me out of belonging, if only in my mind, which is enough. Years ago, my uncle saw me barefoot and said, "I'd love to have those big wide bear paws!" He said it admiringly but looking down at my "bear paws" pressing heavily into the wood kitchen floor, I flushed. I was maybe ten when I couldn't play-wear my mom's shoes anymore, and somehow that day encapsulated something horribly wrong about me to myself. I was just a child, but I had outgrown my own mother.

A handsome military doctor once held my feet in the White House infirmary. I was spending a semester of law school as a clerk in Obama's Office of White House Counsel. That day, in keeping with the rest of the internship, should have felt rare and exciting. But anxiety about my feet dragged me out of the moment's headiness—what it was like to get up from my White House desk, get a bottle of White House–branded ibuprofen from the first-aid kit, then get permission to leave my memo on presidential power unfinished and visit the doctor's office down the wide, curving wood steps. The doctor came in the room, realized he forgot his pen, and left to get it. I almost left, too, despite the ripping pain in my ankle, because he was white and tall and polished, and I was afraid my long wide feet, which he'd have to touch to examine, would displease or bother him. I started to sweat. My pulse picked up. If he noticed me freaking out, he ignored it. He sent me home with an Ace bandage and ice and orders to wear sneakers to work for two weeks, which I did not do; sneakers make your feet look bigger.

Did you know that when you go into Payless, and sneak to the size thirteen women's aisle after pretending to pause in the size ten aisle, all you see are big Black women? It's the same at Nordstrom Rack. Why we statuesque, thick women of African descent have big feet, I don't know. Is it Africa, or miscegenation? Maybe our feet come from a robust gumbo of West African and Scottish and English and Native American blood and are unique to us in human history. Maybe they are an adaptation to standing all day in fields, hard at work and watchful, in rare autumn snows and dependable summer heat, or to running toward self-liberation. Maybe our feet survived because we, and they, were the fittest.

If I'd grown up with the Black and Mexican side of my family, where plenty of us are pudgy with stone-heavy bones and everyone's brown and nobody's white, I'd be less messed up about this. I might see my feet as a connection to my ancestors and their ingenious survival. But I grew up with my WASPy family, with ceaseless diet-and-binge cycles and forced trampoline jumping before dinner and no one, nothing, that reflected my body kindly. I went to an all-white school and, in second grade, had to announce my weight to the class every Monday so my little white school friends could help me make better choices in the lunch line. My mother, who is white, grabbed my fat and said it would kill me, or no boy would ever dance with me, let alone like me. My feet became the location where these lies about myself—which I took as truth—rested.

"Hand me your plate," Holt said, lifting a burger. Silently, I did. I was smiling, but whatever confidence I once felt, or fun lust I once signaled, had disappeared. Fear replaced it. The place behind my solar plexus tightened. I chastised myself for my wishfulness—as if Holt would choose me, smart and witty and even pretty as I was, upon seeing through my feet just how completely I differed from the fetching white girls I presumed he dated (at least one of his exes was white, and petite, and cute; I'd seen a photo). This was the danger of pursuing the white male gaze: if it landed on you wrong, it hurt.

Holt wasn't the first white guy I'd tried getting close to in order to game the social hierarchy. It never went the way I wanted it to. Years before Holt, whom I met in law school, there was Tucker. We were undergrads studying abroad in Italy. Tucker had a shag of blond hair falling across his fore-head and a pack of Camel cigarettes flip-flipping in his fingers. He was tall enough that his blue eyes looked down at the top of my head from his Lacoste-and-Top-Siders perch. He was in a band, voted liberal, and laughed easily. We smoked joints in my living room, lay back on the scratchy brown couch, and I got much higher than him though he smoked much more than me. We drank beer and spritz at bars in the piazza while he glanced, confidently and continually, at my braless chest. He took me to see the Dave Holland Quintet in a dusty, golden town outside Florence, and I remember pretending it was a date, which it may have been. Beforehand, we ate hard-boiled eggs and caviar at the linoleum kitchen table in his apartment across the Arno. The sun was low and fell across the table, our food in a slab of goldenrod light. I'd never had fish eggs before, and he cracked a joke about our meal being from a Baby's First Caviar kit. This delighted me—that he felt comfortable referencing caviar around *me*, that I was "baby" and he was orienting me to his world.

Back in America, we stayed in touch. Tucker was from Connecticut but spent time in New York City, where I lived. He could be pushy—I remember him telling me that, as a boy, when his nanny wouldn't give him what he wanted, he peed on her coat—and I accepted his mild coerciveness as if it were an overture to my transformation. At a party on the Lower East Side, I sat on a bed, blurry and bobbing from liquor and leaning torpidly against the headboard, when Tucker walked across the dark room and sat beside me. "Hey," he said, smiling. "There you are." "Hi," I answered. He pulled a joint from his pocket and lit it; his arm touched my arm. "Want some?" he asked. I said nah, and he asked again, and I said no. "Come on," he said languidly, laughing, his face very close and his eyes on mine. "No, really, I'm drunk enough." "Here," he said, and, not moving his eyes, put the wet end of the joint between my lips. I felt his fingertips press more and more firmly on my mouth and I inhaled, though I didn't want to. I wondered if he would kiss me, if this was it, the moment after which I would no longer have to be me. He didn't, and it wasn't. Quite the opposite. Soon, he'd snort coke with my girlfriend in a bar bathroom, and they'd hook up and spend half the night together. She was a film producer's daughter from Manhattan with long golden hair she flat-ironed, pale skin, a little waist, and boobs that were like perky water balloons. I felt, at last, the wrecking ball of certainty that Tucker didn't want me. I had not fooled him.

Henry was a white law student with a velvety buzz cut who took caffeine pills and talked a little bit like Chandler from *Friends*. He was senior to me in the Obama campaign, where I worked after college. I drove him home one night and could tell from the looks on our colleagues' faces that they thought we were going to hook up. The freeway was empty and we sped to San Francisco. As I leaned over the pool table at a bar below his apartment, I felt his hand slap my ass, then grab it. Because I wasn't cool, wasn't the kind of girl who knew what to do, I told him "Stop!" like I actually meant it. Later, drunk, we sprawled across his floor mattress. There was a moment of quiet in which he popped up and walked barefoot to the kitchen for a long swig from a bottle next to the sink, and then another. When he came back to the mattress his lips and chin smelled like fresh scotch. He got up for another sip a few minutes later. I remember thinking, *But we've already brushed our teeth* . . . I felt the curdled energy in my gut say, *I think he's an alcoholic*. Outside, the North Beach bars kicked their last patrons to the foggy sidewalks, and wasted hollers mingled with the sounds of idling trucks and Spanish-speaking delivery guys. Henry whispered, "Pull the blinds." He curled his arm around me and stroked my arm and the side of my stomach. I felt the familiar, thrilling mix of nerves and possibility—*this must be the beginning of him seeing me as a suitable girl*. He ran his fingers along my arm, along the dip of my waist, down to my fingers, back up to my shoulder. I was turned on and hopeful, full of a throbbing buzz, but I was also tense. For the transformation to happen, he'd have to have access to my body—but not full access. I'd have to somehow conceal the telling parts, like my feet. I stayed frozen with my back to him, staring at the wall against which the mattress was shoved. I wanted him to touch me more daringly, decisively. I also longed for the freedom that might enable *me* to do the same. But I was too afraid of offending him. Eventually his hand stopped its slide, grew heavy with the relaxation of sleep. And that—that nothing—was it. The next morning, he said, "Hey, I'm sorry about last night, it was just instinct. You were a warm body." I hadn't asked, but I interpreted the comment as a signal of morning-after mortification. I replied, "No worries."

That summer, I met Blake in the law firm kitchen where secretaries brewed coffee and lawyers filled their cups. I was a summer associate, and he'd already finished law school and been at the firm a few years. He wore San Francisco–slim khaki pants, brown suede shoes, bright yellow socks, and a crisp pink button-down shirt with Burberry-checked cuffs. "Too much, right?" he said, looking at the fabric on his pale, hairy wrist. "I'm gettin' razzed for this shirt. Time to give it to Goodwill." He was muscled and beautiful in a creamy way, Caravaggio's *Bacchus* years later, running up the BART steps with a five-o'clock shadow and weekend-surfer's tan every Monday morning. He seemed to come from money. He had backpacked or cycled on nearly every continent. He had gone to Harvard and Stanford. Philanthropic with a lusty appetite for food and wine, he taught me to use Maldon salt and he published op-eds about public policy in places like the *Wall Street Journal*.

Whatever those couple of months with Blake were, they ended sour and nasty. Before it ended, though, it took the same intoxicating, baffling form as so many of my relationships with gleaming, ticks-the-boxes white guys: we played a quasi-romantic, chaste, not-quite-right version of house that never ascended from the runway. I wanted them to want me, and to change me. (They wanted me for something, too, but more on that later.) We had dressed-up dinners at smart restaurants; we talked on the phone until batteries died; we had pet names (Skivvies, Cafecito, Bookie, Savalita); we shared forks and toothbrushes; we watched movies under blankets; we spent weekends together, starting with a Friday-night sleepover and ending with Sunday brunch.

We never even kissed, but once we were in this odd dynamic, people doted and cooed like they do around young love. The guys sometimes leaned into it. A deli owner handed me and Henry our paper-wrapped cheesesteaks and, looking me over pointedly, said to him, "You're a lucky man, my friend." My heart raced. Henry smiled and didn't correct the assumption, and neither did I. Meeting me at the parking lot beside his building and tossing the familiar attendant a twenty for my overnight stay, Henry said, "He thinks we're fucking, don't you think?" I didn't answer. Was this an invitation? A worry? A fear? The limbo exhausted me—the sense of being allowed in, but not wanted. Or wanted, but not allowed in. I slept at Henry's apartment so often his roommate, who generally slept at his girlfriend's house, asked how long we'd been dating. I said, "We're not." But I said it in a way that left room for interpretation. That night, we watched *Rosemary's Baby* and gossiped about campaign volunteers. My bare feet were on his lap. He rubbed them for a minute but it seemed halfhearted. It was excruciating! I barely breathed and didn't enjoy it and couldn't pay attention to the movie until he paused (or was he done?) and leaned forward to grab his Tecate, at which point I moved my feet under the blanket.

Blake and I once had dinner at a fancy restaurant we both wanted to try. He made us a reservation for a Friday night and we drove there in his car. The waitress asked us where we wanted to sit and I said, "Anywhere, surprise us"; she walked us through the dark, Pacific Heights restaurant, a blur of mahogany and gold light, tinkling glasses and low chatter, to a section where each small table had one loveseat instead of chairs, so Blake and I ate our exorbitant, egg-topped burgers side by side, legs touching. When he stretched before dessert, he put his arm around me. The waitress arrived with our cake and said to me, "You're so pretty, by the way." And instantly, for just a second, I broke character, flashed my cards: I whipped around to Blake and cried, *"See?"* as if we'd been fighting about whether I was beautiful—him saying *No, you aren't*, me saying *Yes, I am*—and the waitress had just proved me right.

We drove to Blake's apartment. From the passenger seat, I moved playfully to grab the manual gearshift as we hit a hill. He laughed and said how frisky I was, grinning. Inside, we lay on his bed while he told me how fit he was, almost too fit to find a challenging workout, he said. He was in basketball shorts by then and his warm, hairy legs were stretched out, his thigh next to mine like a golden rock. Should I touch it?

Did he want me to? I got up and went to get lip balm from my purse. Bent over and rummaging, I felt him come up behind me, laying his body on top of mine and sighing, resting his stubbled cheek on my back. (This was one of the most awkward and inscrutable physical encounters I've ever experienced; I felt both like a table he was resting his exhausted body on and a lover about to have rear-entry sex.) I slept over, but on the couch; we'd started a cryptic European movie and at some point he said, "I'm exhausted," stood, and walked to his bedroom. There didn't seem to be an invitation to follow him. A moment later he called, "There's blankets in the hutch!" The sense of being allowed in, but not wanted. Or wanted, but not allowed in.

Not long after, we had dinner in a Financial District bar. Slanting into me with heavy, buzzed affection and scrawling his name on the receipt, he sighed and said, "Oh, the day will come when you'll hate Blake Williams . . ." I didn't respond, but it plucked me out of the foamy reverie I was lolling in beside him at the bar. The next week, I met him at his apartment after a day of moot court competition (a debate team for law students). I took a quick shower while he answered work emails and fried us eggs for dinner. We made salads in mixing bowls. Mouth full of greens, he said, "So my friend is coming up next weekend. Where should I take her?" "Your friend?" "Yeah, well"—he put another forkful in his mouth—"friend is the word I use. But I need someplace romantic." "Ah," I said. He chomped his food. "So. Any ideas?"

I remember sitting at Plant Cafe with a girlfriend, the brackish smell of the bay and shrill seagull calls in the air, and going on and on about Blake and the "girlfriend" development, energized by my own confusion, by his alternating warmth and chilliness, by my parallel certainties that he was into me (his behavior) and that there was no way he could be into me (my appearance, my identity, his behavior), by how he reinforced, maybe unknowingly, my googly-eyed longing and then elbowed me away. I insisted to my friend that my confusion was not unfounded: that same night he asked me where to take the girlfriend, he also gave me a CD of slow, swinging Rubén González and one of his oldest T-shirts, thin and blue and fragrant with his body.

I met this girl a couple weeks later at a birthday party. She was like a doe, quiet in the bashful way of Jackie O, with a delicate, small body. Her snow-colored prettiness had the precision of a porcelain doll. She had brown hair that lay across her back and shoulders in smooth waves and she kept her purse on her lap. Her skin had the color and poreless clarity of a peeled egg. He didn't introduce her, but I learned her name was Olivia. When they went to the bar for drinks, she clutched his hand.

About a week later, we had a halting, uncomfortable goodbye at his apartment before he took a cycling trip to Argentina. Nothing triggered it, per se—it wasn't *goodbye forever*—we just stared at each other for a long time in his doorway, not talking, or we said good night but didn't close the door, didn't walk across the landing to leave the building. I drove home watching a plume of fog move through the Bay Bridge spires, wondering how much longer I could stand this suspension. Blake called the next morning on his way to the airport and left a happy message about how much fun we'd had the night before, the trip he was about to take, and getting together when he returned. I called back right away. On his voicemail I told him to have a great trip, that I'd see him soon, and, stupidly, "I wish I'd kissed you yesterday when we were saying goodbye." He didn't call back. But I got a long email from Argentina—the spartan hotel, the snowy mountains, the decent food. The last line was, "Also, got your voicemail. Thanks for saying that!"

I want to think that, if I'd been capable of directness, of expressing my own desire forthrightly, and of deeper confidence, I could have had actual romantic relationships with any of these guys. This might be delusional. Henry, from the Obama campaign, once told me he could only date girls who were shorter than him; I was an inch taller. After finding Tucker, the friend I met in Florence, with my girlfriend in the bar bathroom, their powdery noses pressed together as they kissed and giggled and banged into the wooden stall, I cried, "What the hell are you doing?" as if I'd burst upon an affair. Eventually, I emailed him to explain my reaction. He never wrote back. When Blake got back from Argentina, he asked me to look at an op-ed he'd drafted before it went to the *Washington Post*. I said I'd pass, and asked whether he could maybe give me a tiny bit of space after I'd told him how I felt about him and he'd rejected me. "What are you talking about?" he barked. I said I felt led on. He asked how, kind of spat out the question, then said I was wandering into the weeds when I mentioned how he'd touch me, or take me to dinner. It was a brutal twenty minutes, after which I felt lacerated. We only talked a couple times after that, exchanging brief, perfunctory niceties at work or social functions. And handsome-footed Holt, with whom this dynamic never got started but perhaps could have, told me before we ever hooked up that he only wanted to be friends. I think he was being honest, but mostly just kind, when he said that he wanted freedom to fuck around unbridled, and our friendship meant that if we hooked up it would be, by definition, consequential. I pinpoint this evening, us two in the doorway, his face a little tortured, my smile accommodating, as the Official End of any chance I had with Holt. But the actual end, at least for me, was weeks earlier when I saw his feet and my self-loathing surfaced, right up in front of my eyeballs where I couldn't ignore it, and I began to shrink away from him into a space I hoped was half-invisible.

Hindsight, between a rock and a hard place: my self-loathing both propelled and doomed these weird, cryptic couplings. My sense of failure, deformation, and nobodiness pulled me toward men I thought could, by their presence and proximity, erase my relentless otherness. Which is to say: fix me, as if my otherness were a pathogen; or erase me, as if my otherness were a mistake. But those same senses of failure, deformation, and nobodiness made me incapable of any sincere connection. Bent on my own annihilation, how could I be present and available? And what did I blame when our connections, always choppy with static, finally frayed and split? My blackness, my bigness, my poorness, the vulgarity I perceived about myself that I'd hoped our connections would erase. But oh, the thrill was real while it lasted. These white guys could make me feel faint just by throwing a lazy arm over my shoulder for a photo or taking a sip from my glass at a bar. Strolling past my office, Blake once winked and said, "Hey, darlin'."* My chest clutched inward, something electric and sparkling filled my head. I grabbed the edge of my desk and closed my eyes, head forward, shocked by the boozy, fast swirl of heat that had exploded in my stomach and was leaping through my body, effervescent and alarming. That night, I told my best friend about the *Hey, darlin'* fizz and she said, "Warning! It means they are bad for you. It means your dysfunctions align in terrible ways."

Here is a fact that seems meaningful: I married a white guy. I resist seeing his whiteness as a prize, though. This is partly because he is not high-gloss, preppy, and silver-spooned in terms of social capital. When I met my husband, he worked the early shift at a GM plant and woke at 4:30 a.m., ate Pop-Tarts and drank a can of Coke for breakfast, and drove a decaying gray Dodge up Highway 75, foam busting up from the seats, a Detroit Tigers cap on his head, classic rock on the radio. He's from Detroit proper. He dropped out of high school. He finished college in his thirties after a decade of night classes. A mechanic from his teenage years, he has still never taken a car to the shop. He rides motorcycles. He's quiet and unaffected.

---

* Twelve years later, this strikes me as unusually warm for Blake in a professional setting. Still, it's what I remember.

He's not flashy or conspicuous. His family has no money. His funny-Valentine, blue-collar, Midwestern roots leaned against his youth in a Black city and made him a different kind of white. One of the first things I noticed about him were pictures of him with his arm around Black guys. I paused, wondering whether this was performative diversity for my sake. "Who're they?" I asked. The reserve in my voice was probably imperceptible to him, though a Black woman would have heard and understood it. He said, "Ronald and Jim, two good friends." It was a meaningful answer, though having Black friends doesn't mean you "get" Black people any more than being a man with a wife means you "get" womanhood. Over the early weeks, I grilled him—had he dated other Black women? Yes. Did his family mind? Not that he was aware of. Did he *only* date Black women? No. How had the other ones worn their hair? A weave, he thought; I was trying to understand what he knew about natural Black hair. Why did he think so many Michiganders stayed away from Detroit? Why was affirmative action unpopular among the blue-collar workers he knew? And so on. Slowly it became clear that there was no possibility of self-erasure through him; he was not blithely living in, using, and gazing at the world from the tower of his whiteness, maleness, and social power, and so his approval wouldn't lift me into that tower alongside him. The hardscrabble elements of his early life, his outsider mindset (Detroit vs. Everybody), and the fact that, for years, he'd been in community with multiple Black people made him a *fit* for me, not a fix.

Seeing the fit wasn't instantaneous. I freaked out to my girlfriends that he'd finished only one year of high school, worked on cars, and rode a motorcycle. "There goes my chance of being First Lady," I'd laugh, but only half-kidding. Yet by the time I met my future husband, I was less interested in the project I'd pursued with Blake, Tucker, Henry, and the others. After I told Blake I wished I'd kissed him, gotten his ridiculous "Thanks for saying that!" reply, and tried to talk frankly with him about the confusing nature of our bond, his anger and nastiness were clarifying. Initially I was humiliated—by my own naivete, by the limitlessness of my only-half-requited attention, time, affection, and energy for him. But then, like a spark, his affronted anger triggered my own. It invigorated and toned my instincts for self-defense. I felt wronged. The smooth entitlement, the hale cockiness of endless upward mobility, the confidence of being the world's protagonist—the attributes that drew me to this type of guy on my blighted quests for transformation—began to repel me. Chasing these dudes was like simultaneously experiencing my demise and ordering it, like an empress who's split in half, her gladiator other-self wounded in the dirt and looking up, her royal-empress thumb turning down. I'd always wanted to be the empress; I was becoming more interested in the gladiator. Still, even today, I sometimes must take my fingers to the sad, groveling, nearly antebellum neural pathways that occasionally insist my white husband *is* a prize, that his whiteness *does* boost me up, and disable them. Sometimes women of color pass each other on the street with their white male partners and smile like, *We did it.* (The men don't notice.) But within the smiles is a tightness, a shame, perhaps, about the fact that they are smiling. I don't want this anymore.

I would, however, like to understand what Tucker, Henry, Blake, and to a much lesser extent Holt made and make of our relationships—in the sense of two people relating—nascent, murky, strange, wishy-washy, and thrilling as they were. Writing about them is a kind of resolution for myself, but it's also a holding out of some too-late, backward-facing hope, as if by revisiting what I remember I can correct it, or explain it, or even understand it. Of course, I know, *He's just not that into you.* Undoubtedly true. But I was not imagining their interest in me, either. I have normal friendships with white guys, where this vexed closeness doesn't happen. I can spot the difference, and there was a particularity to my bonds with Tucker, Henry, Blake, and the like. Were they drawn to, and maybe simultaneously away from, what I represented with my brownness and bigness? With how my class background potentiated my Black body? Were they drawn to something motherly, to using my soft, brown femaleness as a tool for comfort? They would not have been the first white men attracted, subtly or explicitly, to Black and brown women in this way; perhaps they, too, are shaped by what they came from. These are ideas I'm too chicken to ponder deeply, let alone ask them; but I think of Henry snuggling me in bed, then saying I was just a warm body. I think of Blake draping himself over me, then getting angry when I brought it up. I think of Tucker's cool fingers on my lips as he firmly pressed a joint into my unwanting mouth. I think of Holt, who seemed sometimes into me and sometimes uncomfortable with that idea. Mostly, though, I think of my own inability to fully let these stories go.

In the unresolvable ambiguity, I choose to believe that these white guys were simply unknowing, not skilled enough to see or manage the complicated net of attractions, crossed signals, and impossibility we created. I choose to believe that they were not consciously using me for physical and emotional caretaking. I choose to believe in the complexity even if I'm the only one who can see it. It's a form of self-protection, an instinct I wish I'd had sooner.

Don't Let It Get You Down

What's it like? Well, it's like a booby trap. Like the wild, unbidden springing of a jack-in-the-box. That's the problem. You want to go about your day. You want to live the mundane and the profound, the diner cups of coffee and the once-in-a-lifetime milestones, without being reminded in that cruel, casual way of what you are, of the lowness of your station. But, no luck. Out of nowhere and everywhere, racism comes roaring up at you, its jaws on your ankles, its jarring face suddenly so close to yours that you gasp. It is always there. Or, it's always ready to be there. Tiny, sometimes. Ambiguous, sometimes. But always. There is never a true reprieve. There is always a robbery underway.

I.

You had to meet my dad and be physically in his presence to see him. Meaning, to understand him. If you were astute, you could understand all of him, in a way, just from that moment of eye-to-eye proximity. If you were not, you understood nothing.

He was tomato-stained fingers and the lithe, limber body of a seven-year-old, walking the leafy rows of *solanum lycopersicum* at the Mexican border, a little agricultural worker in small sneakers, bits of dried bean and tortilla on his cheek.

He was solitary confinement, and he was also the six-by-nine-foot cell in which he sometimes lived with another inmate, a toilet reeking of someone else's urine and shit inches from his pillow. He'd ironed his clothes by spreading them under his mattress at night. He made toilet paper by ripping apart paper bags and rubbing the pieces until they became soft. He taught me these tricks as we sat in his hulking, dented Ford pickup. Before he'd begin, he'd light a cigarette and the smell would waft through the truck's cabin. I loved the first scent of nicotine in the air (and, because of its association with these moments, I still do). I loved the time with him, though I was ambivalent about his stories, what they signaled about him, and what they signaled about me.

He was Black. He was a three-hundred-pound body, but he was not fat. He had big hands and feet, like me. He had prison tattoos of naked women that blurred and became brownish over the years, almost the color of his brown skin, and an eight-inch knife clipped to his belt. He was brown eyes filmy in old age, a jolly, wide grin. When he was happy and excited, his voice shot high. He charmed truck-stop waitresses and soft-handed nurses and spoke Spanish to busboys, though he called the language Mexican, because that's what he was. He could only bear-hug you, with his wide shoulders and six-foot-four body.

Which of these things did my baby daughter sense when,

right after my husband and I moved from Michigan to California, he arrived at the door of our Oakland apartment to meet his granddaughter for the first time? His beard was a messy tuft of black and gray, his sweatshirt smelled faintly of dust and sweat, the skin on his cheekbones was patched dark from diabetes. His eyes were twinkling and his face beamed with a grandparent's joy, and a father's. He clutched his drug-store cane and cried out, "Gemma! Gemma!"

She was nine months old. I had her on my hip. Her lower lip jutted out and she made a sound of fearful protest, digging her fingers into my skin. I bounced her and said into her ear, "It's Grandpa! It's Grandpa, Gemma!" She was scared.

Is it because he's Black? (As the song says, *Looking back over my false dreams, that I once knew. / Wondering why my dreams never came true. / Is it because I'm black?*) Because he's still a stranger, only visiting now and then? Because his voice is loud, a strepitoso cascade of pride and excitement? Does fearing a Black man or dark skin start as early as nine months? We do learn it somewhere, sometime, don't we?

Sitting in the living room, Gemma stared at my dad with her blue eyes. When he leaned in to tickle her curls and say, "Hiii, Gemma!" she clutched me closer. He leaned back, away from her. "Does she do this with other people?"

"Yes," I said. "It's just because you're new to her still."

She, in fact, did not recoil from strangers. Tears came to my eyes, but I smiled and jangled wooden keys in front of my baby. "She'll warm up."

She did, eventually. Crawling to his falling-apart, Payless

sneakers, tugging his sweatpants, and pulling herself into a stand, her neck stretched back to look up to his face, her fat, golden feet like vanilla pound cakes on the hardwood floor.

"Want to hold her?"

"No, no, no. That's okay." He looked away, into the kitchen, where my husband was making coffee.

"Oh, come on!" I cried.

"Nah. I don't want to." He said it nonchalantly, as if declining a cup of tea.

I recognized it. It's what makes me yell, "Stop it!" when my husband puts his arms around my waist and makes like he's going to pick me up. I'm heavier than I look, my father's daughter, and I'm terrified of the humiliation I'd feel if my husband tried but could not lift me. That gesture of affection, and the freedom-filled feeling of your feet in the air as you're held, is for other women. It's not for me, just as the freedom to exist without carrying others' projected fear was not for my dad. He was, I think, afraid of mortification, of the unique agony of being embarrassed in the presence of those who matter most. A husband who can't pick up your body, or a grandchild who recoils from your body—these experiences are worse than the stranger-induced embarrassment of, say, knowing you scare the woman in the elevator, whom you will never see again after the doors open and she rushes out.

"Really, Dad, she's fine. Let me put her in your lap." I imagined her shrieking as her little body landed on his leg. Still holding back my tears, I set Gemma down on my dad's old-man thigh.

He kissed the top of her head. "Hiii, Gemma!" he said. "Hiiiiii, Gemma!" and kissed her head again.

II.

My wet curls fell to the linoleum floor as the crisp sound of scissors circled my ears. I stared at my reflection: round face, thicker than I prefer, what my girlfriend referred to as "pregnancy cheeks," though they apparently lasted long past delivery. Green eyes, smallish but bright and clear. Skin, a color that matches foundations with names like Sand and Honey. Broad freckled nose and broad shoulders. No figure is flattered by the plastic tarp they drape over you at the salon. Mine seemed especially sad—pyramid-like and fleshy. What I call "Walmart body." Turning my face from side to side, feeling naked as a wet cat, the sleekness of my head as Oliver trimmed my dripping hair was unusual to me. Normally, my hair is large and ebullient. I never see it wet and stripped of volume for long, and I looked strange and naked to myself.

"Whatever happened to Teddy?" I asked, making conversation.

"Who?"

"Teddy, wasn't it? Your old assistant? Long blond hair, super skinny."

"Oh, you mean Terrence. He went and got fat. He's thicka then a Snicka now. Anyway, he's not here anymore."

"Ah."

I turned back to my phone. Oliver is slim and stunning like a ballet dancer and olive-skinned and Black, with two mixed daughters and two big-boobed, white ex-wives. I'm awkward around him. I've known him for fifteen years but he still greets me—greets everyone—with a quick nod of his feline face after his eyes run you top-to-bottom in a queenly way.

I tried to connect once again, pointing to a photograph of Lupita Nyong'o's gleaming, black visage, selling Lancôme and proudly, too. "Isn't she gorgeous? She can pull off short hair."

"Mmm-hmmm. You would never see her in a wig or weave."

"No. It wouldn't look right."

"Okay? If you put a wig on her, she's ho-hum." And we found our conversational stride, so I kept flipping through *InStyle* and we talked about who looked good and who looked bad.

At the magazine's last page, my guard was down. I was happy. Smiling, I set it on the counter and tapped the *New York Times* icon on my phone. "Cleveland Officer Will Not Face Charges in Tamir Rice Shooting Death." It was December 28, 2015. A few days earlier my daughter had opened her first Christmas present, sitting rockily on the floor of our cramped apartment that smelled of teff bread and exhaust from the restaurant and thoroughfare below. It was a few days before New Year's, when my husband and I would be asleep early, never sipping the cold sparkling cider we had bought for the occasion.

I pictured Tamir Rice from the video we all saw, playing in Cudell Park, the footage black-and-white like a negative. *It's probably fake, but you know what, he's scaring the shit out of people,* said the woman who called 911. There was a wooden gazebo, picnic tables, and snow on grass. An old-style cop car driving fast, slamming to a stop. I imagined the pink arm of the officer as he lifted his gun. The whole thing took two seconds. (One. Two.)

"What is it?" Oliver asked.

"They're not going to prosecute."

"What do you mean?"

"They're not going to prosecute the officers who killed that kid. In Ohio. The one with the toy gun." I was staring at the headline but, trembling with anxiety, I couldn't remember Tamir Rice's name. "You saw the video, I'm sure. It was the one where it was two seconds?"

"Hmm," he said. "I think I saw that."

It's hard to describe how the particular resignation of American blackness sometimes feels. It swallows sound. It's an impassive reflection in the mirror, so massive you must look away. It feels like stopping time and disappearing, sliding through that tiny rip you used to press your eye to years ago, when you were little, but what you saw made no sense: candlelit ships bobbing on still Atlantic waters, the hedge of New World green at the horizon, the smell of sex and menstrual fluid and pus from somewhere, and is that the sound of a violin?

I couldn't read the article. But I thought of Tamir Rice, and how Black boys are seen as men, not children, their childhood metaphorically stolen before it is literally stolen. And Black girls, too. I thought of my helplessness, the creeping certainty that there is no way to rehabilitate the past. I thought of fake cigarettes in Brooklyn and Eric Garner and his spotless white T-shirt, and loud music pulsing from a red Dodge Durango in

Jordan Davis's Florida, and cigarillos in a shoplifter's hand on a hazy security camera tape, of Renisha McBride, a lost woman shot on a Michigan porch, and of invisible fire climbing the walls. Like a nightmare I had, where my throat had been slit and I needed help! But my throat was slit so I could not ask for help. *What is wrong with you people? Can't you see the fire? Can't you smell it? We are going to burn alive in here!*

"Hey, now," Oliver warned, "don't let it get you down."

I didn't answer.

"Come on, now," he warned again. "It's just how the world is. Don't let it get you down."

Something about Oliver suddenly seemed older. He's ageless in the way of many Black adults. Is he thirty-five? Fifty-five? But in that moment his years showed. I remembered him once telling me how his grandma and aunties would box his ears if he ever made the mistake of placing their handbags on the floor. I pictured the living room, an arsenic-and-old-lace Southern space, dim sunlight through the windows, pretty patterns on the fabric. He was from California, not the South, but this detail didn't matter as I thought of him then, as he summoned a blend of reserve, weariness, and capitulation that seemed centuries old, as if it dated to and grew from our oldest memories of being in this place, America.

III.

There's this thing where moms of color with light and white-looking kids are mistaken for nannies. It's never happened to me. My daughter and I look a lot alike and she says

Mommy constantly. But once, at our sweet local park where the playgrounds and swings are bracketed by tennis courts and a baseball diamond, we met people who would become our (sort of) friends and I was nicked in a similar way. I was pushing Gemma on the swing when a mom followed her toddler to the other swing. The mom looked white. She was pale with ringletty red hair, like her daughter, and was tall and bird-boned with a wide, Julia Roberts smile. We got to chatting. She told me she was a nurse, pointed to her husband over there, said they were from Oregon. "What about you, where are you from?"

"I'm from Marin."

"Oh, Marin City?"

This is not something she would have said to a white person. Marin City is the public housing project inside otherwise-wealthy Marin County. There's an Outback Steakhouse and a Target in Marin City now, but when I was growing up, it was a sort of bruised valley, a barnacle of poverty on the wealth of the county. Not just that—families made and make homes there, pride and joy lived there, there is wholeness there. I worry my gaze is too white, or white-infected, to render Marin City honestly—meaning, to describe the full shape of it—but it *was* the projects, what you'd call a ghetto. It was isolated and dark, crammed up against the eight-lane freeway that fed the Golden Gate Bridge, ringed on the other side by a dark crescent of hills. It was always loud and fumey, and the hills were on the west side so the sun dropped away from Marin City before anywhere else. It had liquor stores, and clusters of parka-clad kids on corners, and the thick gravel of broken headlight glass underfoot. The light in the building hallways and on the outdoor balconies at the end of the hallways was painfully bright, a stinging, ulcerative white, thin and ghastly, rubbing onto faces and cinder blocks like sandpaper, illuminating the apartment buildings strangely, like power plants or industrial moonscapes instead of homes. Marin City originally housed workers who built ships during World War II. When the war ended, and the shipyards grew quiet, white residents moved freely, as if on gentle breezes, to the rest of the county with its green hills and ocean views, but Blacks, oh the Blacks, who'd come to California fleeing the putrid South, could not. They stayed—had no choice but to stay, literally could not legally leave and so had to stay—in the freeway-side, dark-first crescent.

So:

"What about you, where are you from?"

"I'm from Marin."

"Oh, Marin City?"

"No. *San Anselmo*. Just because I'm Black doesn't mean I grew up in the projects, lady. *Dumb BITCH*."

"Oh my god." (She grabs the chains of her daughter's swing, looks around for her husband.)

A pot will eventually boil over.

"You wouldn't have said that to a white person. You said it because I'm Black, and when you see Black you think *the projects*. Do you know that about yourself? You think you're different, incapable of dropping your blindness and privilege on other people like birdshit. But you're wrong. You're shitting on me right now. And I'm supposed to smile, play along? No. So, nice meeting you and please fucking leave. Go away. Go!"

What I did though was, I smiled lightly and said, "No, San Anselmo." And we pushed our fair kids, mine with a freckled nose and hers with a chinny grin, both with ringlets riding the air behind them as they swung in and out of shade.

IV.

I was driving home from work when the brake line on my red Chevy Blazer snapped. I was at the top of a hill. I pressed my foot on the brake to slow, and nothing happened. I wondered if my foot had migrated to the gas. No. I pumped the brake pedal until I hit a cinder block wall at fifty miles per hour. My seatbelt failed. I opened my eyes and noticed my knee looked like a raw, jacked-up hamburger patty. My chest felt sledgehammered and my face bled. In the hospital, they wrongly diagnosed my knee as a flesh wound when my patella was actually cracked in half. A plastic surgeon was around to sew my nose bits together, leaving only a faint scar. Through grinding jaws I told a nurse I felt agitated and jumpy, like I want to rip off my skin with my teeth, and she put a sedative in me, saying it was a reaction to the pain medicine. A few weeks later, I drove to the hospital to pick up my records. The ER intake form described me as a "large Black female." I was shocked to see myself described that way—it was an accurate description, but the words, in this culture, had a violence to them. Taken together, they lowered me nearly into a grave of irrelevance. I tumbled that phrase around, my stomach tense, an inchoate shape of dashed dreams taking shape in a corner of my mind. *Large Black female. Large Black female.* I knew what

America makes of large Black females, how little regard it has for us. If that is how the world saw me, if I was never allowed to escape it, if the reminders lurked everywhere—even in a doctor's cursive at the bottom of a note—then perhaps I was doomed.

V.

And then there was the specter of Mammy: uniquely American, the original au pair (imported from Africa, or simply the slave quarters), the original domestic, big and Black, occasionally brash and sassy yet always, somehow, docile and content, centuries old and still living in my body. I have wrestled with her my whole life. How she loomed! Squeezed into her bright-blue silk dress, the fabric with no give rippling at the bust seams, her thick fingers dipping french fries slowly into ketchup, staring into space, a bulwark of a woman, her very body an affront. She was the joke, the dread, the fear, alone in the diner. Did she fit into the booth? Or was that table cutting into her stomach so hard it hurt? (Poor Mammy! Even sitting peaceful and serene in her blue dress, there the caricature was like a trickster ghost around her neck: that sassy wagging finger, that neck pumping left and right like a deranged chicken, that angry voice, that bursting-sausage body all full of attitude and know-how and the beastly ability to bear all burdens.) She saw the blond guy and noticed his naked heels in leather loafers, those heels digging in, his friends pushing him on with their pink palms at his back, snickering their little-boy giggles as he resisted. He must have lost a bet. She's the joke.

Or is she something else? Maybe she isn't sitting in a diner, eating quietly. She's in the country, chomping grass, inviting sex as cluelessly as a sheep tail-up in a field. Maybe he could imagine it, his naked feet, her body a waterbed beneath him. Ugly and so very not-white, but there, between her titanic thighs, there was still something worth finding, if only in the dark.

She heaved. Her breasts too huge for beauty. Her breasts more like the barrel udders of milking cows than anything that could be cupped tenderly by lace or hands. That goddamn Mammy *always* alongside me. Up the stairs. Up the hill. *Stop breathing so hard!* I'd tell her. Huffing along, as puffed up as a blimp.

And if she is real, and she lives in me, how do I get away from her? Do I smother her? Lug her dead dark girth through the dirt like cans on a dog's tail? Into a ravine filled with ivy and moss? At the bottom, only the deer with their sweet noses and dainty legs will see her. I will say, *I'm sorry, Mammy*, and maybe someday I'll cry.

Or do I costume her up? Teach her how to walk: light steps, ballet flats. No high heels, never; it's *be a pretty girl*, not a giant. It's *be like a white girl*, not a bulldozer. Teach her to lie about shoe and bra and dress size. Teach her to smile and high-five and agree. Teach her so well that she says, in honest disbelief, "No, they're not!" when, years later, a lifetime away, in a Brooklyn boutique with stacks of thin silk and cotton and a fig tree in the window, a saleslady offers her a different blouse to try because her shoulders are so broad. I could will that transformation. I can do that, and with less blood on my hands. No one dies, no one kills, gets shoved into the deer's valley; I just teach her to hold her breath. Be cute. Be peachy manicures and diamond studs and lip gloss. It really does make a difference to suck in your gut, Mammy. Well, almost a difference. Almost pretty. There's a limit to what costuming can do. Stop breathing so hard. But it's better than it was before.

And if someone asks *Who's that?* or guesses that she's inside me?

Who do you mean? I'll say. *I don't see anyone.* If anyone asks, then that's what I'll say. *Me? God, no. That's just the specter of Mammy.* If they ask, that's what I'll say.

VI.

It's hard to describe how the particular resignation of American blackness sometimes feels. If only you could stop time and disappear, sliding through that tiny rip to which you pressed your eye years ago, when you were little. What you saw made no sense to you—it was the past, yet you were the present: candlelit ships on Atlantic waters, the so-called New World green at the horizon, sex and menses and rotting flesh, and is that the sound of a violin? Yes, many violins. Played for entertainment above deck, played for sorrow below. Played so loud, for so long, that we'd continue to hear them even if they stopped. Played for the men like my father, who had to wonder whether his blackness intimidated his own grandchild. Played for Black boys and girls, gone too soon. Played for the mothers of these children, played for Black motherhood, and Black mothers trying to be civil and polite under the belittling glare of white assumptions, played for the Black women who raised their employer's kids, and the fat Black women who were flattened into caricatures to sell maple syrup and movies like *Gone with the Wind*. We are in a haunted house, living and dead crammed head to toe. We are tied to the house and the ghosts are tethered to the house, too, and when they fly out the windows they look like black kites. There are so many windows, and so many kites. This house is so massive that you must look away.

White Doll

My mom gave my daughter, Gemma, a white doll, and I seethed. The doll was a pudgy velour newborn with a piglet-colored face, opaque blue eyes, and yellow-yarn hair. Glancing at my husband, I suppressed my instinct to take it away. I didn't want to ruin the moment. So I let my daughter play with the doll, squishing and rocking its body and grinning up at me. I sat silent and still and smarting at the dining room table, unable to take the doll, unable to open my mouth and speak, as if my hands were suddenly covered in papercuts and my mouth full of fallen-out teeth.

The doll repulsed me because it erased me. It was like I was outside our living room looking in the window, and instead of seeing myself in this family scene, I saw a white woman in my place. After all, the only child whose first doll should be white is a white child; my child, though she has a white dad and is light-skinned, is black because *I* am. I am her mother. This indignance is about self-respect, and also pain; I am the blackness in Gemma, and my blackness made it that much harder for me to create and birth her. This white doll took my body, which slogged through this country's racial hierarchy to make and deliver my only child, and expunged it from the record. My pregnancy and Gemma's birth were bad enough that, though I've always wanted a big family, I can't imagine being pregnant or giving birth again. I'm haunted by the loss of this dream, and by the fact that race is part of why I lost it. So I want *credit* for surviving a racialized pregnancy—probably the only one I'll ever have. I want a warrior's welcome, I want to be held and healed, not to be slid out of view by a doll that suggests, however subtly, that I'm not here.

It started with worry, a mesh of fear that defined every day of my pregnancy: I worried about getting UTIs; the pain of labor and delivery; whether my husband would be a good birth coach; defects and anomalies; unwashed lettuce in the salad bar at Whole Foods; undercooked scrambled eggs and French toast in restaurants; whether the monitors they wrapped around my belly hurt the baby; stillbirth; breastfeeding (Were my boobs changing enough? How many calories would it burn? Had I bought enough nursing pads and nipple cream?); the baby shower and what size dress I'd be wearing; whether my thyroid dose was high enough to prevent late-term miscarriage; whether I would weigh three hundred pounds by the time I gave birth (actually, not metaphorically); whether the nausea medication I finally agreed to consume—a pricey compound of vitamin B and Unisom—was safe.

In my last trimester, my heart started racing irregularly for hours at a time and I'd get light-headed and sweaty. One morning, my husband and I drove in freezing rain to the ER because the thumping in my chest was so frenzied. I had mentioned these episodes at multiple appointments with my (white) midwives and (white) ob-gyns and my (white) endocrinologist. They said it was nothing. "Your body does weird things in pregnancy." I felt they were wrong; the feeling was a ripple of intuition in my gut that moved tightly. It wasn't just anxiety. It had a soberness, a foreshadowing quality that my anxiety doesn't.

They dismissed me—*your body does weird things in pregnancy*—as they would again when they waved away my concerns about something else, too: a vomit-inducing pain I'd get in my upper back a couple times a month. The pain and vomiting were so intense that I'd drop to the floor when they started, writhing and wailing and puking until, fifteen or twenty minutes later, it passed. We told my nurses and doctors. They had no ideas, no suggestions. They ran no tests. They told me to go home and try Tums. When I threw up the Tums, they told me, inexplicably, that the Tums had probably caused the vomiting. They told me it was stress. They said to try chiropractic—maybe my ribs were out of alignment. We went to the ER again during one episode because I feared I was going to die; the (white) nurse raised her eyebrows, looked at my boobs, and told me I should try a more supportive bra. The episodes continued.

In labor, my jagged heartbeat appeared. My pulse was 175 as I lay resting, hands rubbing my belly. A nurse brought me a Styrofoam cup of mint tea that tasted like plastic and a vial of lavender oil to smell. After an EKG, a cardiologist entered the labor and delivery room and confirmed what I had intuited: the racing-pulse symptoms I'd had for months were from a heart

condition. He'd just diagnosed me, sort of—he suspected ges-
tational atrial fibrillation but couldn't confirm it wasn't a different, lethal problem without more tests—and those tests would
have to wait because I was in labor. I was crying, but he ignored
that, staying light-hearted and upbeat. He said, "We hope it's
a-fib. If it's a-fib, that's mostly just a pain in the ass." In any
event, he said, they were transferring me into the cardiac ICU.

I cried as my bed wheels squeaked down the bright, white
hallway. The cardiac ICU has the same sterile, unmoving chilliness of a funeral home. Bodies are curling inward, becoming
unavailable to life's in-and-out exchange of energy. Around
me, dozens of elderly white men lay with their eyes closed
and dry mouths hanging open. They set me up in a room with
glass walls that faced the nursing stations; I looked nervously
at my husband. "Am I going to be facing this glass wall?" Eventually a nurse stood on her tippy-toes to tape up a sheet. But
I could not shake the thought of Sara Baartman—the "Hot-
tentot Venus"—and how, in the 1800s, her body became a
spectacle under the white gaze of science, how a British doctor
forcibly displayed her at London's Piccadilly Circus while she
wore feathers and greeted onlookers, how, after her death, her
genitals were displayed at a Paris museum until 1974, six years
before I was born.

Doctors came and went, crowding into the doorway. "Everybody's heard about you, a lady giving birth in the cardiac ICU!"
One told me what would happen if my heart raced so fast that
I passed out: they'd have to shock me, and it would hurt. He'd
never done it to a pregnant woman. Lab technicians stuck needles in my hand for blood draws. Nurses leaned on the wall,

watching me groan through Pitocin-fueled, back-labor contractions. One of them said I was graceful. At the time it felt like a compliment. Now I recall it and my stomach crunches in anger. A dozen cords wrapped my torso and disappeared into the machines that surrounded the bed. The machines emitted an agitating hum and frequent beeps. They continuously measured my blood pressure, heart rate and electrical activity, and blood oxygen. They monitored Gemma's vital signs but kept losing them as she moved. I was not permitted to eat or drink. I couldn't sleep, and could only move briefly and awkwardly or I'd disturb the machines and wires. This continued for over twenty-four hours.

I remember frayed, sharp-edged things from the morning Gemma was born: the doctors at my feet; the Black one exhorting me to *Push!*; the heat before fainting getting tighter around my head; the ice-blue fluorescent light; my husband's expression contorted and twisting with emotion; someone saying, *Do you want to feel your baby?*; reaching down and touching her crowning skull—tangible! Miraculous!—and thinking of the wet swirl of curls on a newborn calf's head; the *slup-slup* of one shoulder and the next coming out of me; her body fat and slick as a seal, and lavender-gray; someone saying, *She isn't breathing*; yelling to my husband, *Go be with Gemma!*; eventually hearing her cry; a resident stitching my tear, serious one minute but goofy the next as he tried to make light of misfiring the needle and thread.

If I were a white lady, a thin one, I believe it would have gone differently. I can't know for sure, but social science supports my hunch. We know medical students sometimes don't believe Black people feel as much pain as white people do. We know Black people are less likely to be given diagnostic medical tests. We know Black women are more likely to die in child-birth regardless of socioeconomic status. So, had I been white, someone might have taken my heart palpitations and my pain-ful vomiting seriously. They might have had the doctor, not the resident, stitch my third-degree tear. They might have let me see my placenta—I begged them to, it was a part of my body, I'd made it to feed my daughter—instead of whipping it away in a biohazard bowl. They might have listened when I asked to see my newborn more than once a day as I recovered alone in the cardiac ICU. They might have diagnosed me earlier.

Six months after Gemma was born I had maybe my tenth of those cratering, concussive pain-and-vomiting episodes, the pain so extraordinary that I peed myself and was seeing double. I waited to go to the emergency room, thinking, as I'd been repeatedly told, it was just stress or muscle spasms, or maybe even a flashback to labor trauma; when I finally got there, all I could do was whimper *Help me*. Once admitted, I was diagnosed with acute pancreatitis, which can kill you, and which, in my case, required urgent surgery. I had been showing textbook symptoms for months. I had been showing textbook symptoms for months. I had been showing textbook symptoms for months.

I want *credit* for surviving a racialized pregnancy. I want a warrior's welcome, not to be slid out of view. And I wish that my infant daughter and I had not been sharing a body while I was being judged by whiteness.

* * *

I resent having to teach my child about racism but I also accept it. I'm her mother. Part of my job is to teach her about her body, and this includes race.

My white mom understood, too, that it was her duty to teach me about race, to get out of her own way as a white woman and find Black spaces for me. I credit her for seeing that, once she and my dad separated, she'd have to teach me the things I would have absorbed automatically if my Black dad had lived with us or if his Black family had lived nearby. It was my white mom who ensured I had the vocabulary to feel, express, and describe Blackness. She made sure I had access to Black history, Black music, Black food, Black spiritualities, Black aesthetics, Black style, and a Black political consciousness. It's easy to read her efforts as contrived, but that would be wrong—they were vital. Without the two sets of Black godparents she chose for me, without the John Coltrane and Earth, Wind & Fire 8-tracks that played in our car, without sitting beside me to watch *Eyes on the Prize* in grade school, without affirming how dishonorable and foul some strains of whiteness can be, she'd have left me unable to gauge racial danger, unable to access Black joy and a Black self-image, and unable to drop into the only groups that will have me—Black people, and, more broadly, mixed people. Still, her pedagogy was imperfect. It had to be.

This is how I started getting my hair braided. I wanted long, straight hair like the white girls in my class, and my mom found a way to give me a version of white-girl hair while still keeping me inside, or at least next to, blackness. She learned about African Safari from a Black colleague. It was a grimy-windowed, dark beauty shop in San Francisco that smelled of oil and incense. I remember excitedly selecting two hair colors, a dark brown and a light brown, from the assorted synthetic strands laid like heavy necklaces under a scratched glass counter. The braiders were African. They spoke a bit of English to me and my mom, but it was mostly pantomime. They spoke to each other, and to some customers, in another language.

Afterward, my scalp ached for days, my cheek flat on the mattress at night because the pillow's pressure was brutal. It seemed an okay price to pay for beauty. When the braids began to settle and gently loosen, I experienced a month of happiness: "my" hair trailed in the wind as I ran, I could lean my head to one side and feel the weight of the braids falling over my shoulder, I could make a swingy ponytail. I felt both very white (long, straight hair) and very Black (braids). Still, my mom didn't know or learn how to care for the braids, or teach me to. My head got unbearably itchy. I resisted washing because of how heavy the braids were when wet. She wasn't sure how to properly dry them, and eventually there was a mildewy custard of dead skin and oil where each braid started. My natural hair grew out so that the braids no longer touched my scalp; some braids fell off; and eventually, when it was no longer tolerable, my mom sat behind me on the couch and we watched television while she used her sewing box scissors to *shhk, shhk* each synthetic braid in half. She used a comb and pick to undo the half-braids, and I helped with my fingers on the ones around my temples, until the dank, grungy, crimped brown plastic was around me like a synthetic swamp on the hardwood floor and only my natural, weightless halo of hair was on my head.

In addition to getting braids, my mom sought ways for

46

me to socialize with Black adults. Black gospel in a rundown church, Black gospel filling the halls—my mom and I joined the up-till-then all-Black Marin City Community Choir. We sang alto and swayed to the piano chords as Ruby, our zaftig Black leader, moved her thick arms and big hands through the air, her ruby-red acrylic nails like Christmas lights. Mom recorded the rehearsals and played the tape driving home. We stopped for Big Macs at the first freeway exit, then got back on the freeway and drove home, the illicit pickles and mayonnaise on our lips as we sang *Weeping may endure for a night, but joy comes in the morning.* We both loved the music deeply. But I can't say being in the choir and singing gospel made me feel more *Black.* It made me feel, if anything, more white. The cultural differences between us (my mom and me) and the other choir members (Black people who lived in the Marin City projects) were stark. I was aware of my skin color, and my poorly done hair, my mom's white mannerisms. But I was most aware of the "whiteness" in my voice, how you could hear it when I sang, too. I was afraid Ruby would ask me to solo and, "sounding white," I'd not only fail a test of inclusion and but also embarrass my mom by revealing that she'd failed to make me Black enough. A version of this happened repeatedly in school. Edgar, the gangly white music teacher with red curls and big, floppy Converse All Stars, assumed I could sing like a seasoned Black gospel singer and always gave me those belty parts, encouraging me to riff and run with a gravitas I lacked. He would yank his head around on top of his neck and furrow his brows, pounding the piano and calling out, "Come on! Really *sing* it!" as I warbled disappointingly.

Though it was part of her effort to give her mixed, Black daughter every advantage, my mom knew my private school created a problem with its wealth and whiteness and segregation. So she joined Operation Give A Damn, a mostly Black social justice group that met weeknights at the Marin City rec center. Being around Black and brown kids was meant to be corrective and therapeutic after my days in a primarily white private school. While the parents strategized on flip charts, the kids ran around the parking lot, full of Domino's cheese pizza and warm Coke. When the sun set, a parent ushered us into a conference room to watch a VHS movie on a wheeled-in television. I always suspected my mom was unconsciously "talking Black" in the next room over, feeling simultaneously at home with and intimidated by the Black adults. I felt the same way with the kids, deeply aware of something shared and significant between us but also aware of something others deemed "off" about my blackness. I'd recently brought home a painting, a self-portrait in acrylic, where I had light skin and brown hair in two braids and blue eyes. It looked like me but it didn't read Black or mixed. Disappointed, alarmed, my mom said, *You look like a white girl here.* Instead of understanding that mixed people—especially children—can and often need to wear different aspects of their racial identities, she worried. And because she was my mom, I worried, too.

Meeting Lionella at the OGAD meetings was a reprieve from those worries, and from the pressures of the kids' room, where I didn't talk right, didn't get the jokes, my hair (always my hair!) wasn't styled well, and, the coup de grace, a white person came to pick me up. Lionella's mom was white and her dad was Black, too. Her skin was peach-colored and peach-soft. Her sable-colored hair was frizzy and plaited in two braids that went past her shoulders and ended in those elastics with gumball-sized plastic beads attached. She was chubby in a soft way, like there was a layer of fleece under her skin. She had a quiet nasal voice and smelled of baby powder, and of the cheap hair products you'd find in the Black Hair aisle at a drugstore in the late eighties, a mix of musk and fruit and oil. My mom would drop me off at Lionella's apartment and we'd run down the concrete steps to be outside, away from the dark rooms and the televisions that were always on. At the bottom of the steps was a patio of dry grassy dirt fenced in with a cinder block wall, and we played there happily.

I can still smell her. I can still feel the softness of her face. Thirty years later and I can hear her voice. She was the first friend I had who looked like me and had a similar family. We bonded over being mixed, having Black dads who weren't around much, not having money, and the pain of being chubby (in a fatphobic culture, though we didn't have the vocabulary for this last part). But we stopped hanging out when my mom left OGAD. Probably a year passed without us talking. Then, knowing I was about to hurt her, I dialed her number. Something must have happened that made me feel bad about my mixedness or my body or my relative lack of money. I wanted to separate from myself, and because Lionella was so like me, I used her to do it. Her phone rang and her stuffy, sweet voice answered. I asked how she was, what she was up to. Then I started lying: I told her my mom had remarried a rich man (his whiteness was implied by the fact that he was rich) and now we lived in a big house with an indoor pool. I told her I was thin, that I'd lost all my weight. I told her I was going to a new private school, where I was popular. I told her we had a new Mercedes. I told her I'd gotten my hair straightened and it had worked this time. Then I told her my tiny white dog was about to run into the pool and said, "Oh my god, I have to go," and hung up.

I don't tend to believe in regrets. Life happens, and in mysterious ways one decision leads inexorably to the next—you don't get your blessings without your mistakes. But I regret that phone call. It was pure cruelty, to both of us. But mostly to my friend.

The hair disasters and choir anxieties and nervousness about my self-portraits were small hiccups; the real problem with my white mother providing her Black child's racial education comes down to the jagged bits of her own internalized racism that she never totally cleaned up. Here's what I mean: my mom has sometimes described my dad as illiterate. Sometimes it's matter-of-fact, and sometimes she utters it almost as a compliment to herself, as an indication of just how "woke" she was after rejecting the staid, classist, at-least-a-little-racist norms of her family once they moved from New England to San Francisco. I remember asking my dad if it was true that he couldn't read, and he bristled, chafing at the question itself or at the question coming from his child. I was confused because I saw him read plastic diner menus and letterboards hung above registers. I saw him peruse newspapers. I have two of his prison books, brown volumes of the Federal Rules of Evidence, and there are margin notes in his tall, lean cursive. I have letters he wrote, sometimes by hand and sometimes with a typewriter. In other words, he was not illiterate. I still wonder why my mom refers to him this way, but I hesitate to bring it up. I figure she must mean "not highly educated" or "not erudite," and the cost of forcing accuracy is too high when I sense white fragility afoot. But I remember an episode of *Oprah* where Oprah looked into the audience, moved her gaze slowly from left to right, and with calm emphasis repeated what her guest had said, using the edge of her hand to tick the air like quarter notes in four-four: "When you shame the parent, you shame the child." I think this is why my mom's illiteracy thing—this untrue story she has about my dad—makes me scream. That part of what she passes me are her own racialized blind spots, and I have to contend with them without her help.

Once, my dad took me to get braids. His presence made me feel at home. His body explained mine to anyone who saw me; I was big and Black like my daddy. Around him, I got to feel like a little girl. He sat in the front of the salon, his knees wide apart and his broad, tall body shifting around for comfort on the tiny pleather couch, flipping through old hair magazines and glancing at me in the mirror. He paid with new hundreds, the bills smooth as cream on the glass counter. Always tender-headed, I'd fought tears through the braiding and sat in stiff, painful silence. As soon as we were in his truck he grinned and looked at me sidelong, with tears in his eyes. In a voice nearly overwrought, he said, "I'm so proud of you, girl, hurting that whole time and you didn't make a *sound*." This was part of his love for me, and it was massive. I'm still nearly crushed by the devotion and pride in his voice, thirty years later. I've wondered why my toughness affected him that way—because he knew I'd need it, maybe. He was in his forties when I was born. He had four decades of racialized knowledge built up and stored in his Black body—from his own life but also from his ancestors, who bore the Atlantic in shackles, toes pointed toward America with its virtue and zeal and cascading horrors. My mom couldn't feel those cellular memories, which are nourished, for better and worse, by our own lives. My dad knew things my mom could not. When he saw me chin-up for hours in that salon chair, hurting but game-faced, he recognized seeds of the grit I'd need to be a Black girl, and he affirmed them.

Eventually, I will have to break the seal, to open the bag and let out the thousand rabid cats and watch them crawl over my child, leaving their scratches and hair and scent on her body. As James Weldon Johnson wrote in *Along This Way* (and Margo Jefferson quoted in *Negroland*), "awaiting each colored child are cramping limitations and buttressed obstacles in addition to those that must be met by youth in general. . . . Some parents up to the last moment strive to spare the child the bitter knowledge." I am that striving, sparing parent. I've never mentioned racism. Gemma has seen Black Lives Matter signs and asked me what they mean; I hedge and say, "It means all people are important." The irony of this response is not lost on me. But she is barely five years old. When I tell her what this country and the world do to Black people, I will harm her. She will begin to see herself as degraded. I want to defend her innocence just a while longer.

Still, I worry I've already waited too long. I think of Drs. Mamie and Kenneth Clark and the famous doll experiment, which is probably the reason *Brown v. Board of Education* came out in favor of integration. If you don't know about the experiment, here's the spoiler: white and Black three-year-olds say that white dolls are prettier, nicer, more attractive, and better to be around than black dolls. Which is to say, by *preschool* kids have already lapped up our infected norms and crooked rules about skin and hair and belonging and value. But the line that separates telling my daughter the truth from protecting her spirit is a maddening one. It's excruciating to touch, like the third rail you stare at waiting for the train. The line moves and thrashes. It weeps and crusts over like something you've picked at with soiled fingers. It's fleshy and crooked, like a seam of haphazard stitches. It's as merciless as the scene in *As I Lay Dying* that still makes me wince: a father choosing to pour wet cement around his son's broken leg, thinking it will help, but creating a cast that locks the rot into his child's body.

Peruse a shelf of children's books about race with me. It's been hard to pick the right starter book for Gemma. The titles mean well but they're like infected cuts—press even gently and you can see, emerging between the words, the pus of our septic history. *We're Different, We're the Same; The Skin You Live In;*

Happy to Be Nappy; I Am . . . : Positive Affirmations for Brown Girls; Something Happened in Our Town: A Child's Story about Racial Injustice; Separate Is Never Equal; Big Hair, Don't Care; Happy in Our Skin; Don't Touch My Hair!; Can I Touch Your Hair?; I'm Chocolate, You're Vanilla; Let the Children March; Chocolate Me!; Brown Boy, Brown Boy, What Can You Be?; Hair Like Mine; Skin Like Mine; Love Your Hair!; Look What Brown Can Do!; I Like Myself!; Mirror, Mirror. Who Am I?

I bought Gemma *Shades of Black*. It gets to the point I need to make for her, light-skinned and light-eyed and light-haired as she is. I first saw it in a used bookstore on Broadway in New York City. I flipped through the portraits of variously hued Black kids, reading. *I am the creamy white frost in vanilla ice cream . . . and the milky smooth brown in a chocolate bar. I am the midnight blue in a licorice stick and the golden brown in sugar. I am the velvety orange in a peach and the coppery brown in a pretzel. I am the radiant brassy yellow in popcorn and the gingery brown in a cookie.* After skin comes hair (*the soft puffs in a cotton ball, the stiff ringlets in lamb's wool, the straight edge in a blade of grass*) and eyes (*the delicate streaks of amber in a Tiger's Eye and the warm luster of green in a Unakite, the brilliant flash of blue in a Lapis, and the shimmering glow of ebony in an Onyx*). I'm brassy popcorn, cotton balls, and unakite. Gemma is vanilla ice cream, cotton balls, and a flash of lapis. This is why I bought her the book. Black will *have* her, like a marriage, in which we take each other under our skins, in from the tentless, rootless, fenceless days and nights of living without blood ties. White won't do that. You can't be any bit unwhite and also white. You're pure; or you're out. I want her to know she has a home in blackness. And I leave the book out so visitors will know something about this family of mine. Gemma has fair skin but Gemma isn't white. *You must know that, because you know me.* Even so, a declaration feels important. We have a lot of white friends and family who may or may not understand Gemma's roots, or may conflate her lightness for whiteness, like, "Oh, but you're not *really* Black." I cannot leave this to chance. Maybe Gemma will be one of those mixed people who feels at home floating in between, who won't feel she needs an unambiguous race-home; but I always felt I did, as if the bucolic, green-lawned, good-natured, liberal-rich hamlet in which I grew up was merely an elaborate cloth draped over a dark alley, a place where you weren't actually safe. Even though you were just walking downtown to buy stickers and sour watermelon gummies, or yanking up your swimsuit before swim class, feet cold on the wet concrete floor, or pulling warm quarters out of your pocket to pay for your bus ride, you had to have a side, a gang, a belonging, for shelter and clarity.

These days, as I've become more individuated from my mother and more at home in my blackness, race separates us more concretely than it used to. I've seen more of the world, and though as a kid I felt like a physical extension of her, I now see how differently our bodies are treated. It's ironic, because she's the person who nudged me homeward to blackness, and without her nudging I might not have that home for my daughter, either. Still, the culture's general impulse toward segregation wants to keep my body and my mom's body apart. In a way, it doesn't want us to be mother and daughter. This was fated from the moment of my conception. I feel it most when I hug her: she seems thin and frail, like a glass of skim milk, compared to me, with my statuesque, thick body. I feel what it looks like to other people: a big Black woman hugging (grabbing?) an old white lady. Hugging her as an adult, I have to bend over, and I make sure my arms aren't too heavy on her shoulders. It's like bending to pick up fragments of something precious—the bond we had in early childhood, before I knew how race could burden our relationship. I gather the fragments in my large hands, aware of a gap that can't be bridged.

That which is brought forth follows the womb: also known as *partus sequitur ventrem*, a Roman legal doctrine adopted in the English colonies—Virginia, specifically—in 1662. You could also call it hypodescent, whereby, in societies with a racial caste system, children take the social and legal status of the lowest-ranking parent. An enslaved Black woman could only have enslaved children, no matter the father's race or legal status. It ensured that Black procreation rarely created freedom, and incentivized the sexual and reproductive abuse of Black women. Over time, the word "slave" and the word "black" meshed, and an enslaved Black woman's child was not only enslaved, but also—simultaneously, by default, by necessity—Black, no matter how fair the child's skin was. There is now a deep variegation and inclusivity to blackness that is unique and nearly cosmic in scope; black comes in all shades. *I am the creamy white frost in vanilla ice cream and the milky smooth brown in a chocolate bar. I am the midnight blue in a licorice stick and the golden brown in sugar.* Without meaning to, the caste system so vicious to Black people ensured that blackness as an entity could overtake whiteness with just one drop of itself; I like to think of this as defiance. *We'll turn you with one drop; we'll subsist on next to nothing.* This is a silver-lining interpretation, of course—it's me making the best of a tragic and sadistic history that continues to reproduce itself. The history is dark but the gift of blackness is not. Black literally survives even when wholly embedded in whiteness: I was Black even in my white mother's womb; I was born with all the eggs my body will ever make, including the egg that made my daughter. This means that while my Black body was in my white mother's womb, the egg that would make my Black daughter was in my mother, too. Seeds of blackness. A white woman carrying two Black women inside her—in a way this feels uncomfortable, like our blackness is derivative of her in some biological sense, but it also feels clever, that blackness can survive and grow within whiteness, or what we call whiteness, in silence and beauty. That which is brought forth *does not* always follow the womb. Black/white/mixed; seeds of each in the other; some will sprout and some won't. The bound-up-ness that exists between mothers, daughters, and granddaughters complicates notions of race, but it's also the other way around.

Either I took the doll to Goodwill or I threw it away. My mom used to throw my stuff out, too. Some combination of needing to keep the house in order and her own motherly jurisdiction led her to dump cups of my tea down the sink, toss last year's paperbacks and clothes into the donation box. When I was living in her house, I hated this. Now I see it differently. A mom has a right to discard what makes her life harder, and what she knows her child doesn't need. My kid doesn't need a white doll. And I won't be erased in my own house; the house I built; the house I clean; the house in which I mother my child, bathe her, cook her food; the house of my stomach and thighs and my back that thrust her into the world through a labor that nearly destroyed me; the house I hold together with my mixed, Black arms. I make a home of my body, for my daughter, again and again. In this way, I submit to her, I create her, I teach her about who she is. There are no white dolls in this place.

Dear White Sister

I spent weeks contemplating whether to bring it up, and how. This dear friend of mine had Instagrammed her feet, in roller skates, gliding through shadow and sun on concrete. She captioned it, "I'ma keep running cause a winner don't quit on themselves #freedom." I thought of her tapered fingers tapping out Beyoncé's words phonetically, with adoration and correctness, "I'ma."

She's been getting into roller derby, this friend whom I've known for ages. I assume the photograph was about her process and determination. The little I know about the sport comes from watching two all-female bouts. The players were a motley bunch, with a sexuality that was both butch and pretty. The lingerie, the chunky thighs, the swirling, slamming speed—it was a refreshing expression of womanhood. I sensed a *fuck patriarchy* ethos in roller derby. I imagine that, at least for my friend, the transformation from spectator to player is about, ultimately, freedom. So, I think I understand the quote: she's going to keep at it, struggle and all. She isn't going to quit because it's worth the downsides. Still, a welt rose behind my sternum when I read the Beyoncé-quoting caption, and I thought to myself, *Those words are mine!*

I feel a peculiar sensation when white people borrow—take—something Black: it's like there's an octopus in my chest, peacefully afloat, when danger suddenly appears. The animal contracts its jellied body and expels a gush of protective ink, then darts away in panic. *Don't belittle "Freedom,"* I hissed inside. "Freedom" isn't for a white girl in the Midwest taking up roller derby. It isn't about becoming a better skater, picking a clever name, finding a sexy-rough costume, learning the rules and lingo. It isn't even about the grit of athletics, or feminism, or grabbing a challenge by the throat and squeezing until it's gone limp in your hand. Unless you're Black, and then it might be. Because "Freedom" is a song for Black women. It's ours, even if it's out in the world.

If interracial friendships are going to be fully authentic and safe, they have to deal with race. In twenty years of knowing each other, though, we'd never talked about race on an intimate level—my mixed blackness and her whiteness and how they bump into each other. Still, in depersonalized conversations about race—current events, history—she'd always been a safe person. When she moved to Detroit, she astutely observed that most people fear Detroit simply because they fear Black people. Sometimes we look like sisters, both of us with kinky soft hair and light eyes. In high school, she was odd and artsy like me, never fully legible to the girls who were polished, popular, and culturally ultra-white, the clique that wore Jack Purcells without socks, drank cans of Diet Coke from straws, and drove old family Beemers off campus with their in-demand white boyfriends. She's Jewish, my friend; I, like a lot of Black people, have a soul affinity for Jewish people, whatever their color, because *they know*.

Still, I struggled to assert the truth to her: that "Freedom" is about *Black* struggle. I hesitated to remind her that it's a song about Breonna Taylor and George Floyd, Dred Scott and Margaret Garner, Sojourner Truth and Fannie Lou Hamer. It's a song about food deserts, redlining, and reparations. It's about Lee Atwater and the carceral state, Charlottesville, and all but one president of the United States. It's about Aunt Jemima, Uncle Ben, and the straitjacket of our anger. It's about dating online ("No Black women, please") and wrestling with the BMI chart, and dying in pregnancy and childbirth at three to four times the rate of white women. It's about dying at three times the rate of white people during the first months of COVID-19, how the economic, political, and social decisions that created this fact are welded to slavery's most fundamental proposition: that Black people deserve the bare minimum, that our lives don't matter as much. It's a song about coming to the bottom of a well and treading water forever. It's about *Say her name*.

It's about the color of the light—a crackling, jaundiced yellow, flies suspended in the antiseptic glow—in the cement hallways of the projects. It's about Patsey in *12 Years a Slave* and the triumphant thrill of Lupita Nyong'o hawking Lancôme. It's about forced removal in Forsyth County, Georgia, and policing in San Francisco.

"Freedom" is about the white partner at the firm with whom I often worked. He was a genial guy, progressive and worldly. But I remember he loathed Oprah with an odd intensity, despised her, found her disgusting and self-absorbed and ambitious, and he said so, more than once and in front of me or the handful of other Black attorneys. I felt pressured not to object because I wanted desperately to belong at this firm of seventy-plus attorneys, where the only other Black women were secretaries, where a different partner, laughing heartily, had recently introduced me not as an associate, but as one of his girlfriends. So I said nothing, and I regret it.

"Freedom" is about my client musing that Blacks probably struggle in law school because there are no remedial classes. It's about Elvis and Eminem. Affirmative action. It's a song about experiments using names like Lakisha and Emily—identical résumés, but Emilys get called for interviews far more than Lakishas. It's about hydroquinone cream that bleaches nipples and faces, and it's about forty years of Tuskegee syphilis. It's about nappiness—there was a photograph of D'Angelo in a magazine, arm raised above his head, and someone said, "What's wrong with his armpit hair?," and the color of dead skin rubbed off on the towel, brown, how it might be mistaken for filth.

"Freedom" is about synthetic braids. And the blond guy who pulled a loose braid off my head and said, "Gross! Did your real hair fall out or is this fake?" He added, "I don't know which is worse." Neither did I. But I wanted my hair to flow in the wind when I ran. I didn't want my natural short puff, which the world gazed upon like a cartooned helmet of negroness instead of a Samsonesque crown of roots and potential. "Freedom" is a song about Vaseline thick on my ten-year-old hairline, the pungency of relaxer, my eyes watering and scalp burning. I wait (tick) wait (tock) wait (tick) wait (tock) for the timer to ding, wondering anxiously, as always, whether my scalp is burning or bleeding. My roller-skating friend has thick, frizzy hair and, like me, has chemically straightened it in an attempt to belong. We share a kinship of hair. And yet . . . whether her hair is frizzy or straight, she's white, and frizzy or straight, I'm Black.

It's a song about asses, butts—from Sara Baartman's degradation to the Kardashians' appropriative reshaping of their bodies. It's about how we came to be colored with such spectacular tones—rape, love, and ocean crossings. It's a song about symbolic annihilation, and Kerry Washington's wet hair as she fucks President Grant. "Freedom" is about the cast of *Friends, Girls, Sex and the City, Modern Family, Game of Thrones, The Marvelous Mrs. Maisel, Succession, The Big Bang Theory.*

It's a song about hate mail addressed to Nigger Pig. Nigger Pig would be me. I'd just written an op-ed about Michael Brown in the *Detroit Free Press,* and this envelope was tucked into my mail cubby, below the Berkeley Law alumni magazine, postmarked from the suburbs. A couple weeks later, a man I didn't know called my office. He was angry and incoherent. He said he'd been driving all night and was coming to see me, he'd be there soon. I called my fiancé and my best friend, asking, "Should I leave? Should I work from home?" My office was on the ground floor, close to both sets of glass doors that opened onto the parking lot. I took the elevator up to the dean's suite and told my boss. She said it would be a good idea to tell the university police, and to head on home for the day, which I did.

It's a song about America, this country I fucking love, and

a lineage that can be traced no farther back than a wooden pier in the Alabama river, as if the miles to Africa do not exist. I hear that pier creaking. And the river *slup-slupp*ing against the rocks. The ghosts are singing a dirge, translucent and facedown in the water. It's about neck-filled nooses. I've never seen a lynching. But I think about the sound of them, what the victim heard and said, whether the branch groaned, whether the wind rustled clothes, how far the spectators' laughter carried. I think of lynchings and see the dull, calloused soles of Black feet hovering above smiling white faces. Last Halloween, a neighbor hung a life-sized ghost from their oak tree. They made the ghost by putting a plain, white, full-skirted dress over the wire shape of a woman. She swayed in the cool, golden light for weeks. October weather made the dress shabby and ragged. Each time I passed, I remembered hearing my Black godfather recount lynching stories from his boyhood in Georgia. I remembered my second-great-grandmother. (Say her name: Laura.) Visibly pregnant, she and her unborn child were shot to death, in her home, by a gang of white supremacists hoping to teach the town's Black families a lesson. This, too, was a lynching, though not the hanging kind. Each time I passed my neighbor's house, a howl took place in my gut. I finally left a note in their mailbox explaining, kindly, that this fake, dressed body hanging from a thick rope in their yard reminded me, and probably other Black (and brown) people, of a lynching. I left my phone number in case they wanted to talk. They took the ghost down; they never called. I've never seen a lynching, but I remember something about them against my will. This is blackness. "Freedom" is about this remembering.

Being a Black woman isn't just about these unfair, painful things, and I'd never trade my blackness for whiteness. This bears emphasis. I would never trade my blackness because it is what I am. But even if it were not, I'd want it—because blackness, and American blackness, is the birth site or the re-birth site of such astonishing artistry, choreography, sound, motion, thought, political creativity, soulcraft, economic en-durance, invention, resilience, and inclusivity. Blackness is the opposite of cultural vacuity; is it ironic that, thinking we were inferior, whiteness banished us to the outskirts only to see us create a culture that is arguably more ripe, rich, and dynamic (and borrowed) than any other on earth? Our contributions to humanity are enough to swell us with pride, and they should and they do. In this way, we are all silverbacks. We are all lions. One of the profound joys of being Black is our persistent diversity. Black goes on and on, and with inherent hospitality, invites you in even if there is only one drop of Black in your blood. (Colorism exists; but that is our business.) Black is as ingenious, resourceful, dexterous, and inventive as a double agent. Black people of all hues, geographies, dispositions, and beliefs can see each other, can switch codes, can perform and improv, and, just as women know something about gender that is often a mystery to men, Black people know more about whiteness—its inner workings; its underbelly; its face without makeup, tabloid style; the wrappers and trinkets at the bottom of its purse; its longings and emptiness—than whiteness may ever know about itself.

Trading my blackness—or my Black womanhood, or my mixed Black womanhood—for whiteness would be an erasure and a bewilderment, not just a switch. In the place of blackness, I'd suddenly be able to bank on some privileges, powers, autonomies, and positive outcomes that I can't now. I'd have fewer calluses and pockmarks, and fewer fears, and fewer abrasions from rubbing against state power. But I would also be home to an emptiness trapped in a terrible paradox: my identity—*white*—would be the taproot of so much unprovoked violence and suffering in my country, yet also the source of my importance and power, and to keep that importance and power, to keep my peace, I'd have to, on some level, acquiesce to the myth of my supremacy and my innocence despite evidence to the contrary. This is a paradox I want none of.

It isn't that white people themselves are empty, and it isn't that white people are violent; it's that the system of whiteness is violent, and if you are white you are part of it, you're in the net, a beneficiary if not an investor. Your hand is somewhere on that sword, like it or not. It's that to become "white," people must trade the deep, thick cultural traditions, flavors, and colorful selfhoods that made them "nonwhite" when they arrived in this country. This is part of what lets "white" often sub in for neutral while "ethnic" means spicy or dark or mysterious or pungent or funny-sounding. In this way, whiteness can seem cultureless. I prefer Black. I prefer holding blackness, in all its tones and timbres, against my chest, letting it be my inky, ancient amulet. I prefer knowing secrets that people who call themselves white will probably never know. I prefer my double consciousness, my soul, my ancestral grid, my nose, my daughter, my grandma, my mixed-Black joy and my chin-up pride to the paradox of whiteness, glorious though it may (unconsciously) feel to be white.

All of this Black happiness and thanksgiving for Black creation was inside me, alongside Black pain, as I pondered "Freedom" and that sticky Instagram post and my feverish, curdled response. Race-life is cumulative; the joys add up, thank god, but so do the injuries. And the injuries are destabilizing. They shove you, knock you, have you bobbleheaded. You're always trying to catch your footing. The injuries lobbed by our Black-hating culture are so doggedly senseless, lopsided, and untreated—the doctor will *not* see you now—that eventually your mind rolls cockeyed in your skull, enervated, and when you gaze inward your eyes rub against a cobwebby fog. Though you walk with a limp, you can't even tell if you've been injured or not. *Is this cut real?*

The other day a white lady stood behind me at a coffee shop and when the cashier turned away from the beans and toward us, he said, "Can I help you, miss?" He was looking at her. "Yes," she said. She stepped around me and ordered her drink. My mouth opened but I was quiet. A few minutes later, when I was finally served, I wandered to the milk and sugar table, coffee in hand, gazing into the middle distance. Sprinkling cinnamon on the foam in a hall-of-mirrors daze, I simultaneously shrieked to myself that the shit happened because I'm Black (it did) and that I was crazy to cry over something so wee, so stupid, just a pebble in my shoe; suck it down, move on, the bile will subside. It's not worth it. Don't cry here, where they'll see you; cry in the car on the drive to work.

That's destabilization.

And that was, indeed, the worst part of this "Freedom" experience: how I didn't believe my own gut reaction. How I shut myself up for weeks wondering if I'd been troubled enough by her post to speak when speaking might upset a white person—moreover, a white *friend*, not someone I could easily walk away from and never see again should the conversation go off the rails. If I told my friend how I felt, would it make her angry? Would I sound crazy? Would I be that neck-swiveling, all-muscle Big Angry Black Woman? What if she had a clever response that made me look stupid, or made me more upset? What if she was defensive and lashed out? Was I wrong about "Freedom"? Was I overblowing things? If this is navel-gazing, it's because they broke my neck.

To be sure that my claim to ownership was valid, I rewatched *Lemonade*. I rewatched live performances of "Freedom." I read reviews and articles about the album. I read an interview with Beyoncé's coauthor. Everything I found corroborated my understanding of the song. How can I be wrong about something that belongs to me?

Fortified, I wrote drafts of emails suggesting humbly that "Freedom" is my song, our song, not her song, and that using it for a hobby, however important, belittled our hymn. I tried to be soft-shoed. I tried to say she can love "Freedom," but maybe not use it. I tried to say it's *sort of* like why white people shouldn't use the n-word. No, not nearly as bad as n*****—unlike the n-word, we can all like Beyoncé—but does the mere fact that Beyoncé's words are public mean white people get to use them as they wish? I chewed this bitter cud for days.

A while back, I read a great piece German Lopez wrote for *Vox*. It showcases Ta-Nehisi Coates's brilliant thoughts on why white people can't use the n-word, and what they might learn from this look-but-don't-touch experience:

> Coates first pointed out that it is normal in our culture for some people or groups to use certain words that others can't. For example, his wife calls him "honey"; it would not be acceptable, he said, for strange women to do the same. Similarly, his dad was known by his family back home as Billy—but it would be awkward for Coates to try to use that nickname for his father.
>
> "That's because the relationship between myself and my dad is not the same as the relationship between my dad and his mother and his sisters who he grew up with," Coates said. "We understand that."
>
> The same concept applies to different groups and their words. "My wife, with her girl friend, will use the word 'bitch,'" Coates said. "I do not join in. . . . I don't do that. And perhaps more importantly, I don't have a *desire* to do it."
>
> Coates added, "The question one must ask is why so many white people have difficulty extending things that are basic laws of how human beings interact to black people."

My friend—more savvy about race than many white people I know—picked up and misused something that belongs to blackness, seemingly without understanding this Black ownership and seemingly without any understanding of the awkwardness it posed, or how it assumed a nonexistent relationship between herself and the material, or how it tore the history off a work of art that is deeply fused with the past.

When I finally talked to her, I focused on this idea of cultural appropriation, that she had taken something that was not meant for her. Bad idea. Maybe because the phrase—cultural appropriation—has a political, adversarial edge that seems at odds with the well-worn, nuanced, *both/and* nature of a decades-old friendship between two thoughtful women. Maybe because it suggests a willfulness, or even a lack of knowingness, that is often at odds with progressive white identity. Maybe because understanding what happened as a cultural appropriation would have forced us to talk about our uneven power. Neither of us were eager to acknowledge that when cultural, social, and political power and value are concerned, she ultimately trumps me. I think we found it equally humiliating and troubling: me saying, "I'm beneath you and you're above me. That is why this hurts," and her saying, with comprehension and the kind of awareness that precedes regret, "So that's why I get to do this—in the hierarchy, I'm above you and you are beneath me." It's not that she is superior to me in any actual, objective way—nor I to her; she was just born with more racial currency. Our baked-in notions about race are the barbed, foundational matrix that wraps our culture like butcher's twine on a roast. In the ultimate analysis, white trumps all. And she is white; Jewish, progressive, probably what we'd call "woke"—but still white.

Through two phone calls and two email exchanges, we struggled. Decades of friendship helped keep us in the room. She reiterated how being Jewish makes her an outsider and how Beyoncé resonates with her. I agreed that these things mattered though they were not, for me, dispositive. She asked what, if I'm right about "Freedom," is a non-Black person supposed to do with their love for the song. This doesn't strike me as a difficult question to answer—love it! Just don't take and misuse it—but in the moment I said *I don't know*.

I had decided to pen an essay about our struggle over "Freedom" and sent her a draft before it ran, reiterating that my intention was to chronicle my experience, not to attack her. When she got back to me, she wrote that, while she didn't object to publication if I wanted to put it out there, the essay was an emotional screed rather than one based on reality and not really about her, anyway. To my dismay, as if it solved the problem, she added that the woman who got her into roller derby was Black. Once I had the final version *Bust* wanted to run—a bit milder, more focused—I asked if she wanted to see it. She said no. I went to her Instagram account and saw that she'd blocked me. Same on Facebook.

A couple of months passed. I called her twice but never heard back. I texted twice but there was no response. About a year later, I reached out once again because we'd both been invited to an important wedding. I emailed, *I know we aren't really talking but I'm ready to be friendly for the wedding day, at least, if you are.* She replied that she wasn't going to the wedding and didn't have the time or energy to reconcile with me anyway.

For a few months, I was philosophical about this fallen-out mess. We simply never agreed with each other on who or what "Freedom" is for. I wanted it, she wanted it, and nobody wanted to let go. We'd been friends for two decades, and though those decades meant our conversations about "Freedom" were tied to old baggage, high school through college, those decades were ultimately a balm, a reason to chill and give each other grace. But time has not healed this wound. To the contrary: my philosophical remove has evaporated. I smell white fragility, and I'm laughing a demoralized, confounded, and bitter sound, like: *How 'bout that! Nice trick. You fired the shot but I'm the one dressing the wound.*

A few months ago, I traveled to the small city where she lives and did not even consider calling her, or arranging a quick visit. If she had wanted to reconcile, I would probably have said no, it's all too far gone. I'd wish her well in the metta sense, with gratitude for the years of good friendship, and maybe even someday imagine we'd add each other back to the holiday card list. But I would not be interested in rebuilding our closeness because I'm not interested in debating the validity of what I absolutely know. And, yet, that's what we did. As if a debate could be restorative. As if we were evenly matched, her atop a hill of racial privilege (and somewhat blinded by that same privilege) and me coming up from a valley. As if the outcome of the conversation wasn't nearly preordained by the terms of racialized life in America. Sensing the futility, I tried once or twice to pivot from factual debate to feelings. I tried to say, *But this right here—your reaction right now—is why I was afraid to bring this up.* But even that was hard to say. I didn't want to draw her attention to her own failing—afraid, again, of upsetting her further; and she showed only quasi-willingness to see the privilege of her whiteness flaring all around us.

This friendship collapsed. There has been no revelation

and reunion. Through the fallout, though, I came to see the sanctity of my intuition. I came to see that defending my Black knowledge is paramount. I can live with this exchange—friendship for sovereignty. Not because I don't miss and love my friend—I do. But because I will not debate what I know to be true. Because guarding the autonomy of my Black mind is the same as guarding my freedom.

I refuse to disappear.

Bad Education

I used to sit on the phone with my best friend, both of us watching dead women in our separate, crummy New York apartments and neither of us talking. So many dead women! We were shown their stiff corpses in repose on icy sidewalks, their long, tangled, days-old hair and exhausted, flopped-out ankles, their knees bent at impossible angles, the bloodstains gluey beneath their cold heads. It never used to bother me, back in the day. Never disgusted me. Never made me nervous. Was never too much. Quite the opposite, in fact: the show comforted me. My roommate and I watched countless *Law & Order: SVU* marathons, absorbing the dead women and the men who killed them, in too much of a daze to turn on the lights as the sun set and the room darkened. Sometimes I think back on those marathons with shame. It's not accurate to say that I enjoyed seeing women brutalized—but it didn't faze me. It was OK with both of us. It was OK enough that we could consume it over and over again, be seduced by its variations from episode to episode, be lulled by its repetition. This strikes me as something like enjoyment, maybe an indirect and more knotty version of it. They made this quasi-enjoyment easy: each episode included the tickling, purposeful juxtaposition of these dead female special victims with the heat of the leads: the lip-glossed, husky, high-cheekboned steeliness and compassion of Detective Olivia Benson, the dense, pent-up masculinity of Detective Elliot Stabler. We were meant to feel their attractiveness; it was part of what drew us into the show, part of what took the edge off the violence and made it edible rather than purely poisonous. In that same period of *SVU* binges, I ended up next to Christopher Meloni, who played Stabler, on the stretch mats at my gym. His eyes were intelligent, his hands roughed-up but well-shaped, his body like one thick muscle, and he was doing crunches by the hundreds. So he was hot in person, too; after this gym encounter, my girlfriends and I would spend commercial breaks giggling and humming about what a long, pointy nose like his could do.

During those marathon days, it didn't occur to me that there might be something strange—or at least worth examining—about my willingness to binge stories of females being destroyed—even if those stories often had a happy ending (for the living, at least). It didn't occur to me that my unquestioning enjoyment of *SVU* might not be a neutral, natural thing, or that it might be tethered to my screwed-up dating habits, my dad leaving us, and the other questionable media and entertainment I consumed. I saw no patterns at all. Nor, for years, did I see how my love of *SVU* exemplified a broader theme in the culture: our collective willingness to gulp down violence against women as entertainment, and how that norm helps to shove women like me, who would prefer to rage against such violence, into a chronic, numbed bardo of normalization and consumption.

* * *

I can't binge on that anymore. I see *myself* there alongside those women, targeted and silenced, and it repels me. I noticed this change a few years ago, after my dad died, when I returned to watching hours of *SVU*, just like I did in my twenties. *SVU*'s formulaic cadence was a familiar comfort, its darkness a fit for my own grieving, gloomy insides. But, unlike before, I could only watch episodes with a male victim. I'd read descriptions and skip the many, many episodes in which a woman is raped, maimed, tortured, or killed. I could no longer gulp down femicide as amusement and diversion. It no longer felt harmless.

I consider this progress. I consider it extremely good that, being a woman, I'm now, at the age of forty, finally less interested in entertainment that draws its life force from depicting violence against women and girls. I also consider my change in taste a return to an intact, unsullied version of myself. Because I wasn't born wanting to accept, let alone be entertained by, seeing women killed. None of us were. That peculiar ability— maybe even appetite, given how much I and so many women will ingest—was learned and reinforced, relentlessly.

It started before I was born, when my mom dated Jim Booker, a short man with pressed slacks and stocky shoulders. My sister and brother called him Jim Booger. They called him Booger because he hit our mom. I don't know what "hit" means because I have never asked for details. I laughed at the story of Jim Booker because my siblings laughed, like, *Booger! What a loser!* The little joke he became and the lingering shadow of him in our lives was a lesson. It alerted me, rather gently, really, to the nexus of danger, men, and women. It said: *Men hurt women.* And, more subtly, *That's not great, but it's part of life.* And maybe more subtly still: *It was a Black man.*

The learning and reinforcement continued: there's a memory in my head in which my dad is strangling my sister. I must have been two, three; she must have been twelve or so. The image is murky. He's hulking and she's small. His hands are around her neck. A warm, autumnal light passes through the green corrugated roof over the deck. Something about the memory is red, like red tree leaves in the distance or a red carpet. My eyes are low to the ground and looking up. My sister's brown hands are clamped around his brown forearms as if to remove them. Her hands are soft, his arms are almost lacy with dryness. I hear a sound of constricted breath. Possibly my own; everyone, including my sister, has told me he wasn't strangling her, he was shaking her shoulders. I believe them, and her, though that's not what I saw.

My parents separated when I was two or three and I lived with my mom. I wasn't frightened of my dad altogether, but I remember being frightened of his anger—his size, his loud voice, the wide swing of his big arms when he gestured forcefully, and perhaps even his blackness, as I was probably already being brainwashed into associating dark skin with danger. Together, the elements of his anger had a sonic-boom quality, like an invisible, physical wave of thunder was plowing through the house. So different than the anger of my petite mom, which could be strong but was static, didn't seem to leave her body and rumble the rooms. I saw my dad's temper more than once. I was probably eight when I called him a bastard. We were driving on the highway. I knew the word was illicit, an insult, and that it had something to do with a misbehaving mother, a mother whose misbehavior attached to the child. I said it, and he immediately yanked the doll I'd been cradling from my arms. He hurled her out the truck window. I saw her head pop off on the concrete. Before he moved out of our house, my sister once did something in her room she wasn't supposed to and, infuriated, he took her door off the hinges; she was a young teenager and the loss of her privacy was a trespass. Another time, he punched the living room wall in anger, breaking the bones in his hand.

I was used to there being a side of my dad that scared me. One I could ever so slightly guard against. But I was never guarded around my granddad, my mom's father, until the summer afternoon when, disobeying him, I learned something about my smallness in the world, and the danger of not listening to a man's requests. My granddad's office was always cooler than the rest of his house and we spent a lot of time there when I visited in hot months. He'd let me sit in the office with him at the linoleum table he used for a desk. I'd color on newsprint as he read me stories from ancient Egypt, the Old Testament. These are treasured memories. Once, though, he wanted me to stop coloring and listen, to listen with full attention, and I wouldn't, or didn't, put the pen down fast enough. His hand clamped on to my forearm to stop it from coloring, and he clenched so hard that he was shaking. I remember his fingertips were silky and the hair on his knuckles was white, and his hand itself was white on my caramel-colored arm. I instinctively dropped my shoulder to relieve the pressure. He let go. It felt as if he became someone else in that brief time, as if a boil of ruthlessness had burst, and before he could stem its flow, the force of it moved his hand.

Outside my family, I first saw the overt nexus between men, danger, and women/girls in sixth grade. One teacher showed us funny slideshows on Fridays when we'd been good and the chart beside his desk was filled with gold stickers. There was always a slide of two animals mating. The class giggled. The one I remember is the elephants, and the male elephant's penis, pendulous and gray and alarming. This was the same teacher who'd pop into the girls' bathroom sometimes because he couldn't keep the girls' room and the boys' room straight. "Oops!" he'd say, snapping his fingers like *I forgot, again!* as he backed out of the swinging green door.

Another learning experience: When I was eleven or twelve and living with my mom and siblings, a handful of skinheads saw our open door, came up the steps, and walked through the house we rented and into the backyard. It was July fourth, my big brother's birthday. He threw a party every year with live music in the backyard and a half dozen silver kegs under the grape arbor. The front door stayed open all night. Hundreds of people came and went.

The open door must have caught the skinheads' eyes. I was sitting on the arm of our new secondhand couch when they came in. There were two or three of them. Maybe four. I was old enough to know what skinheads were and what they represented. They wore work boots laced tight, black jeans, and white T-shirts. One had red suspenders. One had a red-checked shirt—like a flannel but not—over his T-shirt. One had a black leather jacket. They radiated a menacing, profoundly entitled edge, an edge made more intense by the disorienting, arrogant smiles on their faces.

They walked through our house slowly, looking at framed family photos and leaving a trace of boot marks on the hardwood floor. The conversations inside the house stopped; the adults around me were silent and watchful as the music and laughter from the backyard continued. It was a tense few moments, and then the skinheads left. They left, in other words, without wrecking anything but the safe and celebratory mood. But they trailed a lesson behind them, too, exclusively for me, the only young Black girl at the party: being Black *and* female, I sensed that I was a uniquely attractive target. A skinhead's hate would find me because of my race, and he could use my gender to make me feel it, either sexually assaulting me or overpowering my young-girl strength. In that moment, I was pushed into a quicksand of hazards and precarity that Black males or white females might never know. It was my first experience of intersectionality, though I didn't have the words for it then, only the sensation of three-dimensional foreboding, of sinking into an isolated confinement.

My education in gendered violence and violation continued in high school, but here it took on a perverse tinge because it seemed we girls were somehow to blame. Everyone knew that Rick, beloved English teacher and would-be poet, once dated a student. Maybe she was a sophomore when they hooked up? We knew Joe, the gym teacher with the curly hair and strangely thin smooth legs, who had only just graduated from Stanford, or maybe used to coach swimming at Stanford, started dating Kim the day after she graduated. These stories were gross, a bit, but we were all a little jealous of Kim and the nameless sophomore, who seemed so desperately wanted; I was jealous, too, because they were white, and their pretty whiteness seemed to be part of why they were selected for this attention, attention that I could not then read as wrong. My private high school was, in some ways, a paradise: soccer and water polo trophies shining in a row; many dedicated teachers who had the ethos of hippies and brains filled with genius; school-sponsored vision quests in Death Valley over spring break; the circular grass lawn where seniors sunbathed in tank tops, Shakespeare's *Macbeth* splayed open on their legs; a multimillion-dollar arts center paid for by the film-director father of an enrolled student; it was progressive and artsy and enamored of conversations about diversity. Behind the idyll, however, roiled violations and faulty assignments of responsibility: these teacher-student "relationships" were open secrets, and the school seemed to rely solely on us girls— fourteen, fifteen, sixteen years old—to determine when sexual attention from our male teachers was appropriate. But how could we? We were kids. And one of our primary functions, we'd been taught, was to be desired by men—this was the message of nearly every film, television show, book, magazine article, and fairy tale to which a girl born in 1980 was exposed. (Recently, alumni received an email telling us that Frances, our sardonic, in-demand precalculus teacher—who was also the director of transportation and safety—had been fired from another school for sexual conduct with an underage student.)

I was twenty-one when these lessons landed, physically, on

my own body. I'd been warned about Luca because he was from Napoli, "a city of con men," they said. He was a slim, twenty-something bartender with chestnut hair and pouty eyes who wore skinny jeans and bit his nails. I sometimes made out with him and he was delirious with lust for me, which I enjoyed. The moment we'd kiss, he'd get the hazy, hungry, half-asleep look guys have when they're getting hard. It made me feel ascendant. But maybe the fifth time we hooked up he tried to put his hand down my pants and I didn't want him to. I'd never done that before with anyone. I kept saying no. He succeeded, though, and his fingers were frenzied and hard like crab legs as he crawled them around beneath my underwear. I kept pushing his chest and protesting. Finally, he jumped back with an expression like I'd spat on him. He walked away disgusted, as I cried and tried to catch my breath, reaching for the phone in my pocket to call my mom. I stopped going to the bar where he worked. Months later I saw him again in a store. His face was so lovely, almost girlish. We made eye contact and I smiled a reflexive rictus, then looked away, aware of my vulnerability and my inability to vanquish my violator, the impermissibility of it. Risk, harm, a dangerous man—though I had been warned.

And then there's the kind of lesson and reinforcement I tend to see now. The kind that smiles at you from the corner of the conference room, chuckles at your back as you take the elevator to the top floor, the kind that sneers as you cash your big paycheck. Not so appalling, not so physical, not such a lopsided display of power. But they are all connected. I'm thinking of the heavyset partner with the white wavy hair and a thick titanium wedding band who bought us drinks at that old-timey bar in the alley, and as the triangular glasses went around, filled and sloshing with vodka, he said, "One for me and one for you and one for you and one for you." Then he lifted his glass and continued, "But you know, martinis are like breasts. One is too few. Three are too many. Two are just right." Ha! Ha ha ha ha.

This is just a handful of the times I've been taught that men and boys can be dangerous to women and girls, and that women and girls should expect it. The lessons reflected and created reality. They depicted what was actually happening, and they reinforced the likelihood that it would happen again as both males and females observe their societal roles, what their freedom, power, or lack thereof looks like. Not all females are violated; not all males violate. But even when we aren't actors or acted upon, we are trained to be observers. This is why I spent so many years enjoying *SVU*, and why I now find my former fandom so problematic. The episodes were useful in that they allowed me to rehearse a potential reality—they reminded me to clutch my pepper spray on long, solitary walks, to keep my eyes on my cocktail at bars. Yet I could only stomach it all— the rapes, the assaults, the murders, the repetition—because I was so used to seeing women get hurt.

SVU isn't the only thing I've used to rehearse my potential demise, and it isn't the only thing I've liked, in part, because I'm acclimated to misogyny and therefore can (or could) find it palatable.

Eminem comes to mind. I'm not a fan. I'm more of a curious and embarrassed wallflower. I wouldn't pay to see him in concert. I'd be too mortified, old fat brown me in a copse of wailing white girls, eyeliner tears running down youthful cheeks, all of them blond, even the brunettes, holding up signs like *I want to be friends with the monster inside your pants* (a picture of which is on Eminem's Instagram page) . . . and even more unsettling, the hordes of white guys singing and rapping in unison, *Attack-tack-tacking a whore with a damn hatchet.* But for a while I somehow had a crush on him, and I used to listen to all of it—cleaning my house, working out, commuting on the bus to and from the White House. *Put anthrax on a Tampax and slap you till you can't stand.* Or: *Nothing will stop me from molesting you / titty fucking you 'til your breast nipple flesh tickles my testicles.* I clocked miles on the treadmill enjoying that song, de-stressing between law school classes, where I was eagerly studying the ways American law subordinates and controls women. Yes, I felt the friction of my cognitive dissonance, but the beat was good, he was so cute, he was so talented. The violence, the sex, the entertainment—it was all of one piece, why bother staring too hard at the seams? Now, when I listen to Eminem, there are maybe five songs I can stand without feeling nauseated. Not nauseated by him—he's on his own journey—but with myself, and the contortions I have to do to feel something even resembling OK about consuming this woman-targeting vileness. The way I have to say to myself, *He's just kidding, don't be so sensitive!*, as if I'm my own Fox News commentator. I can't stand the dissonance anymore. It's unbearable. And that brings me relief: at last I'm returning to a pre-indoctrinated state, a state I occupied naturally as a very young child, before I'd been asked to accept my own harm as an unavoidable, even entertaining, thing. This particular past—the past I occupied before the culture began feeding me its misogyny and telling me the only thing I could do about it was laugh, was to be a good sport—is one I'm thankful to revisit, at last, with my life half over.

My blackness is now on guard against misogyny, too. As I've matured, my blackness and womanhood have merged not just as a matter of internal identity, but politically. It bothers me that Eminem only gets away with this perverted drivel because, of course, he's white, and his skin is code for innocence and normalcy, which works to take the edge off his violence. I struggle to imagine Common, Kendrick Lamar, or other Black rappers successfully singing to such a massive (white) audience about raping a teenage girl, then adding, *Why not try to make your pussy wida? / Fuck you with an umbrella then open it up while the shit's inside ya.* That Eminem's whiteness—a mere fortuity of genes—produces this nonsensical free rein ought to have always pissed me off; for years it didn't. Better late than never.

SVU, Eminem. They were part of a pattern in which I played out and tried to make sense of the anti-woman lessons I'd been learning for years, exploring or maybe rehearsing the type of sexualized violence I thought I might one day be (re)subjected to. So was dating. For about a decade, I was either trying to snag high-achieving white guys whose acceptance I hoped would make me more acceptable to the culture (its own kind of violence against the self)—or I was attaching myself to guys who scared me. Like my pursuit of straight-laced, Polo-y white dudes, my attraction to rough-edged, drug-using ex-cons who did not have their shit together was, more than anything, a manifestation of what I'd learned about myself—most important, that my body and my self were appropriate sites for terror and injury. That if I was going to experience love and romance, perhaps it had to be through that lens.

Del had been in prison. I knew it before he told me. I knew it emotionally before I knew it consciously, the information surfacing in one of those blurry, peripheral pockets of clairvoyance we all occasionally have. Eventually he told me himself, then asked if I still wanted to see him. I was afraid, but I said yes. I worried about the wounded instability prison can knit into people—I saw it knitted into my dad—but I was drawn to him. On our first date, we saw *Ray* and ate pancakes with fake syrup at a Brooklyn diner. After the waiter brought our cups of clinking ice water, I got up to swallow a Xanax in the bathroom, as I would on all of our dates. I was only twenty-four; it didn't occur to me that my anxiety wasn't something to medicate but wisdom I should heed. Instead, I thought the goal was to calm myself into accepting the risks of dating him, a newly paroled, far-from-sober young man with, based on his conviction for burglary, the capacity for ignoring others' boundaries. The Xanax worked. I had fun. We talked about high school. I described my black-nail-polish days, buying cigarettes from the vending machine on Fourth Street, filling my coup de ville with two-dollar gasoline and listening to mixtapes of Rage Against the Machine. He talked about flunked pop quizzes and crushes and football from the first two years, and then the next year, brutish and hazy, half-remembered hilarity circled around blunts, strong-arming girls in nightclubs for the cocaine in their tight jean pockets, parking lot fights that ended in bloody faces and shirts, and the burglary that incarcerated him.

On our second date, Del suggested we walk through Battery Park, which was dark and deserted on a chilly evening. I half-wondered—in a fuzzy, shaded corner of my mind, where instinct and irrational fear are hard to distinguish—whether he was planning to assault me. I took a Xanax and held his hand as we walked. It turned out there was a restaurant on the water he'd wanted to take me to, and the only way to get there was to follow the path through the park.

For our third date he wanted us to get on the ferry and cruise through the harbor. I looked at the deep water and the empty boat, and the far, silent lights of Staten Island, and my lower intestine turned to mush. I said I got seasick, felt guilty for lying. Then I secretly opened the pink plastic pillbox in my purse, pretended to cough, and chucked a crumbly, bitter Xanax into the back of my throat. I worried whether he would taste it when we kissed.

The fourth time, we were eating bad nachos in a no-frills, fratty bar near Union Square and Del told me about "Patty with the Fatty," a middle-aged lady with a big butt who lived across from juvie and gardened while the boys were in the yard. She wore threadbare leggings and made a slow show of bending over. He laughed at the memory, how tantalizing her ass was between the chain-link. It sent a pulse of fear through me and I took my pill, pretending it was allergy medication. It was crowded and a white guy next to our booth lurched into my shoulder. He said, "Sorry! Sorry sorry sorry," with a hapless smile and liquorish breath. "It's okay," I said. I gave Del a look like, *That guy's wasted.* Del flicked the base of his beer toward the drunk guy and said, "Hey, watch yourself!" The guy didn't hear. Del called again, "Yo!" The guy turned around, big eyes merry and clueless. He said, "What?" kind of laughing. Del said, "Don't knock into my girl." The guy was still smiling but his smile was turning queasy. "Hey, sorry, I didn't mean to. Seriously." The guy glanced at me. Del jumped up and raised his beer bottle over his head. "Yeah? How 'bout I break this fucking bottle across your face?"

I don't remember quite what happened then (the beer, the Xanax, the cortisol). There were no broken bottles. I assume I made us leave. I know I did not panic. I felt I knew how to handle it. Something about his violence was familiar, as if I'd rehearsed it, which, more or less, I had.

Soon after, we had a fight about his general recklessness. Del paced my Carroll Gardens hardwood floor and I sat akimbo on my cheap IKEA couch, crying. He said he had to leave, I begged him not to. Again, it felt like something I'd rehearsed. I begged him to stop snorting coke, to take his drug tests and parole officer seriously. He paced and paced. I felt I knew where it was all going. When he finally slammed the door behind him, I listened to his feet pound down the three flights of walk-up steps. I listened for the building's metal front door to close. The next morning, on the phone, he told me he left because he thought he was going to hit me if he stayed, which I already knew.

A few months after we broke up, my phone rang. It was Del. He'd been arrested and was waiting to be processed. I wondered why, of all the people he could call, he was calling me, his ex-girlfriend; what kind of endless availability I had signaled to him. He said they hadn't told him the charge because they don't have to when you're on parole. He said they came to his house early in the morning, searched drawers and closets, pockets and pillowcases. They told him to take off his shirt and they examined his body but didn't say why. The next day, I learned that the girl he was suspected of raping said she cut and stabbed at her rapist with a knife. They were looking for scratches.

I think he was probably innocent; when I saw him two weeks later (*I actually agreed to see him two weeks later*) the first thing I said was "Lift up your shirt." He pulled up the hem and it was delicate in his fingers. I didn't see marks, scabs, or bruises. The accuser said the guy spoke Spanish. Del didn't speak much Spanish. His aunt said that when they told him the details of the crime, Del cried and said, *I'm not a monster.* But still, I can't be sure.

Seven years after Del, in law school, I was still at it. Still trying to live out what I'd been taught by our tireless, thorough culture. Still sorting through the entanglement of lessons that signaled I, as a woman, was almost by definition unsafe. I dated Cody for six or seven months. He was tattooed and solidly built, with white, beautiful teeth, warm eyes, and a history of passing out, high, on public transit and pawning his mom's stuff for drugs. When I broke up with him, he protested and cried and said this would probably end his sobriety. I'd never fully trusted that he wasn't using, and it was easy to imagine him using or relapsing into an unhinged, broken-hearted hysteria. When I upset him by ending things, the fear I'd shoved down throughout our relationship started to clang and rise. I became so afraid that I bought alarms. I spent an afternoon peeling the shiny wrappers off their sticky backs and pressing them to the windows in my bedroom, living room, and kitchen, testing each one to make sure it would wake me if he showed up high at three in the morning, demanding to get back together. He never did; though having learned so clearly the male potential for violence, I still, twelve years later, hope I never see him again.

I started therapy after Cody. I was thirty years old. I wanted to get married, and married to a healthy man. It had become clear to me that I was the common denominator among the men I dated, I and my bad education.

But nothing is simple. Violence still sometimes gets me, though in a different way. Not long ago, I stumbled across Chris Brown's "Loyal" music video and got hooked. I told my best friend I was obsessed and she cut me off. "No. A wife-beater complaining these hos ain't loyal? You've lost me." Fair enough. But replay, replay, replay. I was enthralled by his costume—work boots, skinny black jeans, a white T-shirt, a black leather jacket, and a red-checkered flannel tied around his waist—which echoed, faintly, what those skinheads from my childhood wore. It fascinated me to see it on a Black body.

And I was mesmerized by the violence in the video, which is subtle but definite. It had, for me, a strong allure. He kicks at the camera lens, which means he kicks at my watching face. Around 00:58 his eyes flash with madness. And, through lyrics and choreography, he objectifies the women in the video so unabatingly that, by the end, it's a complete mutilation, almost a dismembering. There's nothing left of them but sexually arousing thingness. Fake titties that want to get wasted. Big booties. Nigga traps. Against my better judgment, almost against my will, I watched.

I knew what I was seeing. It grossed me out. I wasn't attracted to what Brown was doing *to the women*, though—I was drawn to vicariously experiencing some of his power. In most mainstream stories, the protagonist's whiteness is a barrier that prevents me from merging with them, living briefly through them. But because Chris Brown is Black, I slipped into him. I dove in, really. Not because I wanted to objectify women, but because I wanted the rapture and exhilaration of having and using the kind of total, automatic power he's reveling in—a distinctly male-type power, a power I fear and revere and am jealous of when, for example, I leave work after dark and hurry to cross the unlit parking lot, squeezing my keys so the largest one sticks out from my fist, a dagger if I need it to be.

I just wanted to feel it. To feel what it's like to express rage after being wronged—and suffer no consequence for that expression. This desire is not something I would've understood or accepted back when I was more interested in complying with female norms; women aren't supposed to crave violent power. That's part of the gender-binary deal. But a part of me does. A part of me wants to stomp a throat. I'm talking about a part that needs justice, that would use violence in self-defense and retribution, like Achilles avenging Patroclus. A part of me wants to indulge my years of fury—and I got to, a little, in "Loyal," because sharing Chris Brown's race meant I could "be" him for three minutes. I got to kick at a *man's* face and diminish *him* to his parts. Let *him* be scared this time. Maybe kick up some red spray with my boot toes, just like they've been doing, those men. Maybe dance in the spray from the throats I stomp, just like I've seen done to my kind and like I've been done to. Picture me twirling around a lamppost, swinging and tapping an umbrella, red drops, *I'm siiiiinging in the rain.* Wait, don't go—this is an upbeat scene! Oh! To feel the spurting, blue-ball release of my own rage! The rage of knowing there was a man who beat my mom; the rage of hearing the sixth-grade teacher's shoes squeak on the tiles of the girls' room; the rage of skinheads in my house, making me a target in my living room at a birthday party; the rage of being assaulted in a nightclub by a man I knew; the rage of boob jokes at my law firm; the rage of having a dad who hit walls and shook shoulders and then left us, left us alone and without defenses against the other men of the world; rage—all of it swallowed and unexpressed because I am a woman.

I was in my office and had just thrown up from morning sickness when the doctor's assistant called. She told me the good news: it's a girl! I grinned, I swelled with love. But in less than a minute I was also filled with apprehension. Because my baby was a girl, she'd have to deal with this violence, too. I'd have to watch her be exposed—meaning, exposed to harm herself, and exposed to other women and girls being harmed. She'd never be free. The violence found me, and it would find her. Five years later, I go into her room to double-check the window locks. I look at her while she's sleeping, her face wondrously soft and ineffable in the night-light glow. And I remember a story: when I was a baby, in a California house darkened by massive redwood trees and beside a flooding creek, the house where my first memories are, a scorpion once crawled *tick tick* up the pine leg of my crib and squatted over me, peering down with twelve eyes, its head under the shadow of its raised stinger. My mom happened to come in and see it. Silently, immediately, she took off her shoe and swatted it. It fell to the floor. She crushed it. She walked to the crib. Made sure I was okay. When I check my daughter's windows and look at her soft, sleeping face, I think of that moment in my own early life, and my mom checking on me in my crib, and killing the danger.

I think, too, of the skinheads who came into our house. Almost more salient than my memory of them is my memory of our open front door. I've read that children who grow up without dads in the home view the world as unsafe. It's as if, instead of a loving bodyguard in the house to ward off other men, an unfamiliar man-shaped darkness hovers outside, and you can't be sure of its intentions. Maybe this explains why, as a child, I always checked the doors before bed, approaching the gold deadbolts with penumbral dread, afraid of psychos on the other side. I then needed my mom to check, too, while I watched. Even now the last thing I say each night is, *Did you check the doors?* My husband answers, *Yes.*

I can't watch the dead-girl *SVU*s anymore. I can't watch the dead-girl movies or read the dead-girl books. I can't listen to the dead-girl podcasts or read the dead-girl articles. I know many women can. Many women make them! And they have their reasons, whether because they are too colonized to see the cannibalization or because they've passed through the vortex and emerged, enlightened, into some post-gendered-violence world that I can't imagine, or something else. But I can't do it. I have shut the door to my mind; I don't want to take it in.

Still (and here I rage, silently), the violence that first found me—the early lessons, the lessons through my twenties—remains with me, careening around my insides, sometimes driving my decisions, often animating my fears. If I think about its presence too long, I panic. It is covered in spikes, and fast, and has many legs. It's like I'm trying to scratch an invisible thing out from under my skin. It's still here, it's still here, it's still here—the threat, the fear, the inevitability. That being a woman means I am violable but not permitted retributive rage. I see this, I loathe it; but I cannot change it. I can't change this reality or the fact that, despite wanting something else, I still have to live it; like the memory of my open childhood front door, and the awareness of a shifty man-shaped darkness always hovering in our yard, leaning toward the house, its face inscrutable and blurred, where my dad, or any kind man—protection, maybe—ought to have been.

To Wit, and Also

I have waited in the inky dark between the trees, watching. For days I've observed the wooden house and the tidy fields, the full barn and the empty wagons. The people, Black and white and perhaps in between. And now here he is, enjoying an evening walk and a cigarette. He is unsuspecting and free. Violet and gold gathers around him as the sun sets. Gray, rich smoke from his own tobacco is in his lungs. He walks and I wait. Not yet, not yet. The breeze stirs. Sweat stings my eyes. He comes closer; close enough that I can clearly see, for the first time, the planes of his Welsh face, the tick marks of gray in his beard. He walks closer to me, closer. I'm scared, but when he is nearly upon me—go!—I fly like a dragon from the thicket of hemlock and pine, landing before him and blocking his path. My hands are in suede gloves. My gun and whip are holstered. I've used no dogs, just my own wits. I point a cloaked finger at his chin and say, "Gotcha." The fear and shock in his eyes! He thought he'd never be caught. I unwind my rope, and begin. I will tie him up and drag him back with me, through centuries and into his future, to be judged.

My sister joined a genealogy website and found a deed in which our maternal fifth-great-grandad, Vincent Glass, gave away his possessions. The inventory included "to wit, one negro woman named Filliss also one named Grace also one negro girl named Peggy also two horses also thirteen head of cattle also ten head of hogs." It was an affront to see people listed beside livestock, but I wasn't surprised that those people existed. I've long suspected my mom's family held Black people captive for forced labor. The pieces fit: old Virginia, white Protestant landowners, racist progeny. The news, when it was confirmed, felt both ghastly and inevitable, both too close and muffled by distance, like hearing domestic violence again and again in the apartment next door and then, one day, the final, culminating thud of a body on the floor.

The slaveholders are my family. I'm a Daughter of the American Revolution, so I've known their names for decades, and I know just how the family tree moves from them to me across five generations. But when we talk about this family history, we tend to focus on the positive. We discuss the men who enlisted in the Revolutionary War, or the great-grandmother who opened a hat shop in Ohio. We talk about the irretrievable American loveliness of those 1950s New England summers when my mom was a girl. They gathered in Gloucester, Massachusetts. She remembers meals around a rough wooden table under a grape arbor, eating fried clams at sunset and surrounded by blue hydrangeas, kids running in the grass and holding open jars toward fireflies. They spent those summers with my mom's grandparents, Grandpa Joel and Grandma Sarah, who were jolly and jowly and—it's offered as a footnote—rabidly racist. (They were born only twenty years after the Civil War, and maybe that partially explains it.)

After we found the deed, however, my mom went deeper, offered more about her grandparents and their views on race. I listened not only to what she said but how she said it: "You wouldn't imagine the fights Grandpa Joel got into with my dad, boy. My dad was liberal about race and Grandpa Joel couldn't stand it. He'd yell and slam the table with his fist whenever my dad would talk about civil rights." She went on to explain how her Grandpa Joel, the one who was proudly racist, disowned her when she married a Black man. "The only advice he ever gave me was, *You better not marry a n-word.*" My mom paused and then continued, "When he died, my grandma changed. She'd been as racist as my grandfather. But then she came to meet Rafael," the Black husband over whom Grandpa Joel had disowned my mom. Eventually, she also met Lotus and B, my older sister and brother, the kids she'd joined her husband in disowning. I refrained from asking what those visits from grandma were like for Rafael or my siblings, the Black people involved, because I wanted to savor my relief: my mom had used the phrase "the n-word" when telling the story instead of actually *saying* the n-word. Occasionally, and despite conversations explaining why they shouldn't, the (liberal) whites in my family sometimes say *nigger* when they talk about other people's racism. They think it's okay because they don't mean it *that way*. They don't taste the blood on that word, I guess, or know that we do. I was thankful that I didn't have to hear it come out of my mother's mouth as she opened up about her family, and I didn't want to ruin it by asking how Rafael or my siblings had fared. Still, I wondered how it felt to suddenly be performing the roles of grandkids and husband for this white relative who, though happily married to a "rabid" racist for decades, suddenly claimed to have a benign and sincere interest in their lives.

I wanted to be sure the deed was real. I didn't want to digest this information—the lives of the white slaveholders in my family, the lives of the Black people they trafficked and held captive—unless I could authenticate it. So, I called around: a courthouse, and the clerk's office in Campbell County, Virginia, and the Library of Virginia, where a lady at the front desk told me the archivist was at lunch. I did a funny thing when I called back: I pretended to be white. This means lifting my voice up so it sits higher in my throat and adopting a kind of upbeat guilelessness. I even used the word negro, just as it appears in the will. I wonder if I fooled the archivist, who sounded white and had a voice and accent as soft and thick as a stack of pancakes. I guess I wanted to meet the moment where it seemed to be: at a fractal crossroads where the racial dynamics of our conversation encompassed the racial dynamics of our country, her with the power of access, me with the desire and hope, and me being polite and white-ish so as to ease her latent fear of race-related anything and to shield myself from the flares her fear might shoot off. I said how lovely it was of her to look up Vincent Glass in the deed books, and just how thrilled my family would be if she found the document. When she called back with the deed book in her hand, I wanted to double-check that the language was there. I think I wanted her to acknowledge it. I asked, "Do you see a paragraph three? Where it says about the two negro women and the negro girl? Slaves, I guess?" I waited, hearing her turn the deed book pages. She made a quiet, tongue-ticking sound that said *Looking, looking.* I held my phone in the crook of my neck and scribbled the names—Filliss, Grace, Peggy, Filliss, Grace, Peggy—on a yellow legal pad, and I pictured myself as a Southern lady, light as a bowl of whipped cream, like how Harper Lee described Southern women: soft as teacakes with a frosting of sweat and sweet talcum. The page-flipping stopped. I listened to her read. She said, "Mmm-hmm, yes, that language is here." I mailed a self-addressed stamped envelope and a check for the dollar-fifty Xerox to Campbell County, Virginia, and waited for a copy of the deed to arrive. It came in a big yellow envelope, the poorly photocopied pages like black-and-white watercolor. I read them once, and it wore me out, and I put them away.

My need to know the details of the family history battled against my reluctance to find out. Over a drawn-out crawl of weeks, I collected images of maps, my nose nearly pressed to the computer screen to read handwritten names of creeks and hills on antebellum maps. Having verified the deed, I wanted to locate the land. We'd had over a thousand acres, tobacco plants in nubby lines like cornrows, the sheds and barns where the tobacco leaves hung, dried, and became cigarette fodder amid the clumpy footfalls and soft, misty snorts of the cows and pigs below. I reviewed land taxes and land patents from the 1700s, processioners' records, and topographical maps—and I think I found it. A satellite image shows our old acres to be green and brown and undeveloped now, bisected by a country road and Rattlesnake Creek, covered in patches of cleared land and patches of deciduous trees. Grainy satellite images are not enough, though; I felt, and feel, pulled to leave my footprints on that soil, to bring some of it home with me, maybe leaves from a tree or water from the creek. This isn't about the Glass family to whom I'm related. I feel no need to visit the land in remembrance of them. This is about Filliss, Grace, and Peggy, who need my family's acknowledgment. I need to bear witness to their lives on the land where they lived, and tell their spirits that I know they existed. It's about my own enslaved ancestors, who, with sorrow, I realize I can only touch through Filliss, Grace, and Peggy. It's a penance, and a pilgrimage.

My desire to visit the land is also about the people my family enslaved whose names we'll never know.

On the phone with another archivist at the Library of Virginia, I said, "But what I really want to know is how many slaves we owned over time. How can I figure that out if I can't trace the actual enslaved people?" She thought for a moment, then said: "I've got it! Property taxes." "Property taxes?" I asked, picturing land and houses. She continued, "Slaves were *owned*. They're listed on each family's tax records along with other assets."

I ordered the reels of property tax microfilm from the Library of Virginia. They loaned them to the library at UC Berkeley, where I work. I started out energized: I walk to the Moffat Library feeling optimistic and powerful, a woman about to confront the past. The security guard waves me in after checking my ID. I take the marble steps in a flash. I arrive at the room where my loaned microfilm is waiting. "Hi, there! I have some film on loan from the Library of Virginia?" I clutch the box, about the size of a bread loaf, and finger the boxes within, each containing a spool of film. I am surprised to realize I've arrived with no pen, no legal pad. My lack of preparation is a kind of avoidance. Unconsciously, I've guaranteed that I can only take cursory notes, that only a bit of the noxious information will burrow into me. I dig a tiny, nearly full notepad from my purse, the one on which I scribble grocery lists at red lights. I borrow a cheap pen from the front desk and open the first box. The reels are glassy and gray, the spools of the microfilm reader creak and whir, and black-and-white images of tax ledgers appear. *Cumberland County Virginia 1798–1816*. The tax books list how many pigs, horses, and cattle each household had. And also how many blacks under twelve, blacks over twelve but under sixteen, and blacks over sixteen. I scan for *Vincent Glass* in each year, and there it is in refined cursive and black ink, the information no one in my family talked about or wanted to face for centuries. From what I saw on those reels, the most enslaved people we held captive at tax time was seven. One year, none. In other years the number varied—three, five, two, four. I'd thought the mere fact of ownership was the zenith of monstrosity, but seeing the headcount rise and fall year to year—the purchase and sale of people disguised in elegant numerals—was freshly and extraordinarily sickening. It scraped off the possibility that this history involves anything but dehumanization. Buying and selling is not metaphorical; it is literal. You can only buy or sell a *thing*. Which, really, is all you need to know about slavery. It is exhausting to see my own black "thingness" through Glass's hollowed-out eyes, and it was exhausting to feel my human capacity for "thingification," too. In the darkening library, my body sore from hours of sitting, my eyes stinging from blue light, I jot the basic numbers down—four in 1797, one in 1798, three in 1799. I leave the library, my head heavy and pounding as if I'd been hung upside down. I have not been back.

I do, however, return to Filliss, Grace, and Peggy, the inventoried women and girl that my family held captive, the only ones for whom there are names. I'm desperate to know who they were, what their interests were, who they loved, to know anything at all about them. I feel nearly conjoined with them, as if we are limbs of the same body, fused to the same thick, white joint. As if when they move, the socket rolls and I move, too. Like we are suspended in a gelatin of collapsed time, the soles of our feet pressed firmly together.

My search leads me to a researcher who specializes in African Americans and our enslaved history. He said even with having the enslaved people's names, it would be nearly impossible to learn anything more about them. The gift deed is from 1804, a time when, he said, a white owner was as likely to record the sale of a slave as I'd be "to record the sale of [my] used couch." If only the date were closer to Emancipation, he said. There'd be more to go on; they might have taken the Glass surname, and the South kept better records of property lines and chattel as the war loomed and unfolded; the better, I guess, to recoup losses and shore up insurance claims in some post-war future. The researcher asked whether my mom would take a DNA test: if she shared DNA with a Black third or fourth cousin, they'd likely be descended from the slaveholding family, and we might find an actual or anecdotal record of Filliss, Grace, and Peggy.

Left with no concrete leads, I've only my imagination—but I'm afraid to use it. I'm afraid the white gaze I've internalized will summon caricatures of blackness, limiting my thoughts to what I've seen in books and movies about slavery that were created by white people. Just as women can internalize the male gaze and then can't help rating themselves as objects of male desire, we Black and brown people can internalize the white gaze and then view our people, our creations, and our very being through the lens of white normativity and white centrality. The gaze makes us ancillary in our own lives, as if we can't exist without measuring ourselves against whiteness. It can be a struggle to see ourselves—and other Black people— as existing for our own sake.

But then I have a breakthrough. Tracy K. Smith, poet laureate, wrote a poem where she talks about a *realm of shades*, and this poem, written by a Black woman, opens a door through which I can see Filliss, Grace, and Peggy, these departed and disappeared Black women from 215 years ago. The phrase *realm of shades* feels inked to them and them to it.

The realm of shades could mean death and the ghosts who linger there; deathly storms raining on the field and dead Black spirits who, after what they've endured, don't have the stamina to return home. That realm of shades now envelops Filliss, Grace, and Peggy. They're gone, and it's been centuries since they lived. They long ago turned away from the brick and mortar of the living world, and maybe death was a balm for them. Or realm of shades could mean the cool, sunless pockets beneath a wide old tree. Not a tree that was forced to endure hangings; a different tree. Under which pine needles touch the soles of their feet gently, the air is a crepuscular blue, and there is respite from a sun that makes tobacco fields skillet hot.

Or realm of shades could be the dark corners of their cabins, where they leave their babies swaddled in Moses baskets. The mothers walk outside and work, listening to their skirts rustle tobacco plants, feeling the grain of the leaves under their fingertips, thirsting for the realm of shades where their babies were, or the realm of shades under the tree, or that death realm—their minds cast backward or forward but never here.

A realm of shades, such as the small shade they made for themselves when they put their hands to their foreheads like visors, and looked in the direction of the rising sun, past the Glass house, past the tuft of woods and the green belly of a hillside, past Falling River and Rattlesnake Creek, to the Atlantic Ocean, which they probably knew by a different name. Europeans and Arab people once called the Atlantic the Sea of Darkness. A darkness that gulps; I imagine them in the split second when there was a chance for escape, sprinting across the decks of relentless slave ships, jumping, and dropping feet-first and straight as redwoods into the black, the salt, the blue, the cold of the Atlantic Ocean, sinking in. I imagine the Atlantic mad and bloated like it says in the Mos Def song, *Fools done upset the Old Man River / made him carry slave ships and fed him dead nigga.* It is the world's second-largest ocean, the ocean into which both the Mississippi and Niger Rivers run and, in my epigenetic memory, a gyre of perpetual, barbarous nightfall, a pusher of hot and cold currents, a lifter of hurricanes, a transporter of ships and their breathing, human cargo.

Filliss, Grace, and Peggy. I can see them through black art. A verse from a poet laureate and a lyric from a rapper help me conjure them; so, too, do bars of jazz from John Coltrane and Miles Davis, the husk and trill of Sarah Vaughan; the vibrant, flowing tiles of an Alma Thomas painting and the thick, unctuous strokes of Basquiat's oil sticks; the pastoral, piquant flavors of Edna Lewis's cooking and her writing, too. Filliss, Grace, and Peggy are still here—if only in my imagination and my longing, if only as shimmers I glimpse through sentient portals of Black creativity.

Those slave-holding grannies and grandpas of mine, I think about them, too. They are effigies stapled to the back of my neck. They beg for forgiveness but they haven't atoned. Instead, they make excuses. They had no choice, they tell me. They inherited their slaves, they say. Who else would cut the trees and bake the cakes and shore up the dikes? Who would dig the ditches and slaughter the animals? It was long ago, they say; it was a different time. Here's my answer: "Odd to be so governed by an appetite." They are confused. They ask, *What does that mean?* I say it again: "Odd to be so governed by an appetite." They look at me curiously but are not curious enough to sit with it, to figure it out for themselves. The night grinds on. It's as if they are constitutionally unable to admit wrongdoing, complicity, darkness, trauma, greed. I leave the room. This is the sound of the door gently closing. This is me pausing in the hall. Will they whine through the night or just fall asleep?

My fear is that they were not only slaveholders, but the wickedest. The kind that liked the blood on their hands and sucked it from their cuticles like sauce. They could have been the type who bound "their" slaves up and sent them South, separating families because they could, shipping them down-river like logs; the type who whacked them like dusty rugs hanging off a porch railing, who broke into their bodies and minds and spirits like a little boy who fingers into the center of a pie and plucks out a cherry. He grins, glancing to be sure no one has seen.

Little boys are not the only ones who sneak around; so, too, do their fathers, waiting for opportunities to exert the ultimate marker of control over the women they claimed to own. Waiting until Mrs. Glass retired to her private chamber, or until Grace was by herself near the well, Peggy had to come to the house alone, or Filliss was caught breaking a rule. I ache for them and the inexhaustible threat of molestation and rape they must have lived under, even when they found a moment of quiet in the realm of shade. Even talking about it troubles me. I don't want to ram these women into the frozen amber of their trauma and leave them there, in our view, forever. But it has to be discussed: there is a strong possibility that the men in *my* family, the old men and the teenagers, put Filliss, Grace, and Peggy in unending peril with their unending appetites for control, appetites that were unchecked by law or religion or morals or convention.

All this is why I say, *Odd to be so governed by an appetite*. It comes from *The Passion* by Jeanette Winterson:

> It was Napoleon who had such a passion for chicken that he kept his chefs working around the clock. What a kitchen that was, with birds in every state of undress; some still cold and slung over hooks, some turning slowly on the spit, but most in wasted piles because the Emperor was busy.
> Odd to be so governed by an appetite.

There are appetites that propel some people to subjugate and tyrannize others. Appetites for clout, for supremacy, for preeminence. And these appetites governed my family. Their bodies, their minds, their vocations, dreams, endeavors—all governed. What a place that farm was, with Blacks in every state of undress; some still cold and slung over hooks, some turning slowly on the spit, but most in wasted piles. *Odd to be so governed by an appetite*; these words pop into my head when I'm overwhelmed by what they did. Its wry and removed phrasing—nearly clinical—allows me to consider what they did but feel separate from it, as if I'm a psychiatrist observing a strange patient. It protects me from experiencing, in my own body, the full harm of their choices.

I have white friends whose families enslaved Black people. Some of them probably owned, some of them rented from other owners. These white friends know because of family stories, or because someone stumbled across an old letter, an old will.

I also have white friends who've never asked. They don't seem to care, or they can't find the strength to wrestle with it. They, like me, come from antebellum families, patriarchs and matriarchs and kids eating biscuits and hog cooked by Black hands (indigo stains, missing fingers, cotton stuck to wounds like gauze). They come from antiques in the attic and debutante balls, Louisiana and Georgia and the Carolinas, such soft names for such scarred land. People enslaved blacks in the north, too, but my family and these friends' families are Southern. So this land I'm thinking of smells like sweet gum and red cedar and magnolia trees, it feels humid and tumescent to the touch, it sounds like the words *cotton* and *sugar* and *tobacco*. It looks like two-story white houses with comely, vertiginous, white columns; you'd have to look closely to see they're made of human teeth. It looks like poor whites, too, living in shacks full of ringworm and watered-down gruel. It sounds like these poor white kids playing hopscotch, still hungry after dinner, always hungry—but at least they weren't Black, and their whiteness was their pride and joy. I and these white friends whose families also had slaves come from the same land. But they've muzzled the past and chained it up like a dog. They don't want to hear it or see it. It's as if their families' reliance on slaves is just an anecdote, as if anecdotes like that can be isolated and sealed up. Their disinterest in their slaveholding history—or at least what I see as disinterest—puzzles me. No, that's too tame a word. It infuriates me; that, though it bothers them when they dwell on it, they seem to waltz through this gilded hall of crimes without proportional restitution and humility, while I and my kin are trapped there. But I take my fury and blow on it, cool it off, let it sink low and settle until I can call it something else. Fury is useless here. These friends and their families can do what they like with their knowledge.* They are good people; people who love me and have welcomed me and have helped me experience life with joy and fullness. They are people who sent wedding gifts and baby clothes. Maybe their relationships to their own history is what we mean when we say "racism without racists." Whatever enlightening water I could lead them to—translucent and bracing—I could not make them drink. I tell myself it's not my business.

And maybe my fury is altogether misplaced. Maybe it shouldn't be aimed at them; most people are uncomfortable atoning for minor trespasses, let alone ones that metastasize and compound, as chattel slavery morphed into Slave Codes, convict leasing, Jim Crow, and mass incarceration. I'm reminded of this at work when, walking to the podium, a veil of public-speaking sweat on my brow, I waver on whether to open events with an acknowledgment that UC Berkeley, like all of the Bay Area, is located on unceded Ohlone land, making it and us occupiers. Most often, I do offer a land acknowledgment, though I'm self-conscious because it is not nearly enough. I don't back up the words with decisive action. I'm not even sure what the right actions would be, though I know that given how massively I benefit from the land theft something is required of

---

* The website Coming to the Table has a twenty-one-page guide on how to atone personally for slavery. It has over one hundred suggestions and is available at https://comingtothetable.org/wp-content/uploads/2019/07/CTTT-Reparations-Guide-August-2019.pdf.

me. Decolonization is not a metaphor.* It means repatriation, and yet I'm not going to repatriate the land on which my house stands. What I am willing to do is study, and sit in a posture of humility and reconciliation,** and give money—and remain aware that none of this, alone or together, is full reparation.

Moreover, if I dwell in fury at a white person who declines to reckon with their family history, I will be furious constantly. After my sister told me about our ancestor's deed, I joined the genealogy site and found the message board. I counted five or six other members discussing our shared connections to Vincent Glass, eager to understand who he was and, therefore, who we were. Here's how I know these other members were white: only I cared about the slaveholding. Only I posted messages and posed questions about it. Whiteness, especially American whiteness, is often premised on amnesia and forgetting, a kind of silent, smiling refusal to reckon with how far into our own lives the traumas of slavery have come crawling. Recently, over breakfast, I told my Black godfather about these indiffer-

---

* From Eve Tuck and K. Wayne Yang, "Decolonization is not a metaphor," *Decolonization: Indigeneity, Education & Society* 1, no. 1 (2012): "Decolonization brings about the repatriation of Indigenous land and life; it is not a metaphor for other things we want to do to improve our societies and schools. The easy adoption of decolonizing discourse by educational advocacy and scholarship, evidenced by the increasing number of calls to 'decolonize our schools,' or use 'decolonizing methods,' or 'decolonize student thinking,' turns decolonization into a metaphor. As important as their goals may be, social justice, critical methodologies, or approaches that decenter settler perspectives have objectives that may be incommensurable with decolonization."
** I'm borrowing this framework of "study, humility and reconciliation" from the nonprofit Planting Justice.

ent folks on the message board. He shook his head slowly. "Imagine," he said. "Being so detached from the reality of your life that you're not curious about your family claiming to own other human beings." I said, "Well, I'm making assumptions. Maybe they've already done their work." He said, "No, I doubt that." When he was a child in rural Georgia, he heard stories of a local Black boy who was lynched; and the Klan once visited my godfather's family, looking for someone (or just someone to terrorize)—all her life, my godfather's cousin remembered the chilling sound of the Klan's cars in the dark, their tires churning the gravel, engines surging up the hill toward the house; and when my godfather was born in the 1930s, the last known person to survive the Middle Passage—a woman who was kidnapped in Africa, transported to America on a slave ship, and sold into chattel slavery—*was still alive*. Her name was Redoshi, but they called her "Sally." There is no distant past. There is only the unending scream of the present. Some people can block the sound. Maybe if I could, I would, too.

When I look in the mirror, the white gaze stands between my eyes and my reflection. The white gaze tells me my body, which looks like my Black and Mexican ancestors, is deviant. It tells me my nose is too broad, my hair too frizzy. I have to hush it, to actively counter it. The white gaze stands between me and how I see other Black and brown people, including Filliss, Grace, and Peggy. I long to see them as they *were*, not how the whiteness that mediates our history says they were. I try to discern them clearly, but a wavy, disorienting film hovers in the way. I try to peer around it, peel up its corners, shiv at the weak spots. But I doubt I can see them, for any sustained period of time, except as confines of slavery. I have moments of clarity—like when I read the Tracy K. Smith poem about a realm of shades—but they are brief, elusive. This can feel hopeless. Yet it occurs to me that Filliss, Grace, and Peggy, for all that they didn't have, might have had this: the ability to live without the white gaze embedded in their own eyes. White people would have seen them through it, but *they* might have seen one another without it. They might have been born in Africa. Or if not them, their parents, or other captives my family held, or captives on nearby farms and plantations, working docks and clearing forests. Enslavement was, unquestionably, a barbaric terror, and it would have infected and injured their vision of themselves and one another eventually—but, if they were new to America, there *might* have been a path of light through which a Black-centric reality flowed. Their subjugation might have been a mystery to them and an outrage, not even a little bit the preordained consequence of natural law, as later generations of blacks, myself included, have been taught. I have to imagine, for them and for myself, a life defined by whole, germinal blackness, their pristine Black livingness. So maybe the Glass family's land was not only the site of depravity and evil, but of women who still possessed their integral, unblemished, left-alone blackness. Maybe it was the location of an un-messed-with, unbroken Black gaze. Maybe there is a realm of underivative blackness there on that land, abiding through long centuries beneath river rocks, beneath bark, beneath soil. Maybe when I visit, I will feel it. Maybe I will jar it and bring it home with me. I would give nearly anything to have it.

State

He remembered his number. We were in an office of bureaucratic plainness, something like a Social Security office, where you go to sign up for benefits or submit something to the county. We stood in a plain white room, at a plain counter. A white man looked over my dad's paperwork and noticed a blank spot, one my dad had not filled. He said, "Do you remember your number?" Meaning, prisoner number.

My dad said, "Yeah," in a voice that was low, and resigned, and hangdog. What I heard in his voice wasn't exactly pride, but there was something satisfied and secretive and sheepish in his eyes, in the way his brow furrowed and he smiled. What was behind this expression? Having the tenacity and genius to survive three incarcerations, years of imprisonment that were indelible and sunk deep into his skin like tattoos, maybe. Or, having the tenacity and genius to stay out of prison once I was born. Maybe embarrassment that he had to confirm, recall, and speak those numbers aloud in front of his daughter. Maybe frustration that he could never escape the imprint of the state, of the California Department of Corrections and Rehabilitation, and half a century later, he still remembered a number first assigned to him as a teenager. Afterward, in the truck, he told me he could never forget it, even if he wanted to.

On my dad's side of the family—the Black and brown side— the state and its violence and power are never far away. It's an intimate, involuntary relationship, always thrumming with potential energy about to detonate. We have had some agency, some choices, and some futures wholly of our own making, I guess—but it often feels like, beneath a thin layer of free will, the state is the decider, the key-holder, the vault from which our limited choices are drawn and into which our histories are thrown, like a mass grave. The state and its extended, strong, pilfering fingers has always had a grip around my dad's family. I wonder what it's like to experience life without the state pushing on you like a battering ram in constant motion. (And then I remember: I can see what it's like to be free of the state: the white side of my family is free, and nearly always has been.)

My dad had one brother and five sisters. They were small children when the state came around, a scythe in hand, to disrupt the family. One of his sisters, my aunt Betty Jo, was nearly screaming when she said to me, "What we remember from that time was that the county and *the state* did that. Look what you did! Look what you caused! Look what you've done to this child!" The state, the state. She was remembering Ms. Hall, the social worker, who would come and check on the house when they were kids. This started after their grandma, Nonni, died and their mom, Hester, developed hysterical blindness. Ms. Hall and her social workers put two of the sisters in foster care; Ms. Hall ("That bitch—what happened to do no harm?") determined Hester wasn't fit to raise that many kids. Ms. Hall told police that my dad was *not socially adjusted* to living in a normal home setting. And quickly, without process, my dad, only nine years old, was taken away from his family home to Camarillo State Mental Hospital. Camarillo was meant for adults, but it took in kids with nowhere else to go. State power, its hand in their house like a flood. My dad's favorite sister, Renee, later went there, too, after she accused one of Hester's friends of raping her ("Which he did!"). The police labeled Renee as "disturbed" and she was removed to Camarillo for shock treatments. My nine-year-old dad was made to assist with shock treatments; not on Renee, but on others, and I picture his little brown hands, which, before Camarillo, had picked tomatoes and pecans and built mud cities in the yard, holding on to someone *like* his sister Renee. When he ran away from Camarillo, he hitchhiked 256 miles back to Brawley, his hometown, only twenty miles north of the Mexican border. He made his way inland through 1950s Los Angeles, Riverside, Palm Springs, and the Salton Sea, which sits like a hot, salinated puddle on the San Andreas Fault. Of losing my dad and getting him back, my aunt Betty Jo says, "What we remember was that the county and *the state* did that." Look what you did. Look what you caused. Look what you've done to this child. The state, the state.

Here's what my dad told me about his childhood home: it was surrounded by fragrant orange groves, and filled with the aroma of his mom's homemade tortillas, and the family owned it because his grandfather built it.

Here's what he did not tell me, but which I learned from his sisters after he died: it was a multigenerational house, with the kids (my dad, his sisters, and his brother); their mother, Hester, who was spoiled, a flapper, and an only child; his mother's boyfriends or, at one point, her husband; and his grandparents (Hester's mom and dad), Grandpa Augustin and Grandma Nonni. As long as Nonni was around, they had food. Nonni ran a laundry business. Businessmen in town said she was the only person who could do their shirts right. They were the first house on the East Side to have a Maytag washing machine. Grandma Nonni's income and will and motherliness held the home together; after she died, my dad's mom, Hester, drank. They had to take in boarders. They didn't have money for utilities. Hester cooked on a little gas two-burner instead. *Abject poverty* was how my aunt Betty Jo described it. "We were hustling just to have beans and tortillas!" My dad was seven or eight when he stopped going to school and started working to support the family. Summertimes, he'd go to the Central Valley and pick grapes and pecans for money. The season ended in the fall and school had already started by the time he got home; he did not enroll. With hours to fill and a house full of need, he picked tomatoes in massive fields for income; a thoughtful, lean boy, his fingers on the fuzzy stems and smooth red fruit. He worked at the back of the market where the produce came in. And he ran away often. Sometimes he rode the rails, a skinny brown hobo kid catching the steamy whistles of trains in his ears and watching America beyond the open boxcar: oil rigs pumping, forests in the wind, poor white people in back-yards, rain turning roads into mud. Sometimes he stayed at the fire station or the police station. He swept them in exchange for a dollar bill or a paper bag of groceries, which he'd drop off at his mom's house, unseen. He stayed at the fire station for over a month and learned to wash the crimson-and-silver trucks. He told them, "I don't have a home." His family only found him because one of his sisters saw him riding in the fire truck as it drove down the street. He probably didn't tell them his real name, Betty Jo said. After his runaways, he'd return to the house and his mother would get drunk, rage and beat him with a belt. *The belt had the buckle. Gramma Nonni would use a switch, but Mom would use the buckle,* Betty Jo said. His mom would yell, "You think you can do whatever you want to do?!" He never put his hands up to defend himself; instead, he ran away again and again. That's when Ms. Hall, the social worker, started coming by.

In the early 1950s, my teenaged dad walked into a bank with a pistol and walked out with over $100,000. He was arrested in Louisiana, sometime later, driving a brown car. There was no money on him, and no money ever found. He didn't want his mom to know he'd been arrested so he told the police he was an orphan. He looked and seemed big for his age, and he successfully concealed the fact that he was a minor. He was convicted and sent to Soledad State Prison, a prison for adults.

For the next twenty years, he'd be released, then go back (San Quentin, Folsom), convicted of other robberies and burglaries. My dad often said, "I operate on a need-to-know basis," and he did. He rarely answered questions about himself—especially about his years of robbing and burglarizing—but he had a sense of humor about his reticence, could laugh at himself and, with amicability, turn your frustration at not knowing into acceptance of his terms. As a child, I knew he'd been incarcerated but I didn't know why. I reasoned that had he done anything *that* bad, his prison sentences would have been longer. Still, I once asked him whether he'd killed someone. This was after my parents separated, and he was visiting us in the house where I grew up, traffic sounds and orange sunlight filling the living room. He said no. This may have meant *not on purpose*, or *not at all*. He must have determined it was something I needed to know. I believed him. The hypothetical I periodically subject myself to—*but what if he did?*—does not alter how I feel about him. He is still my dad, clunky cell phone clipped to the neck of his T-shirt; big self-defense knife on his belt, like a 1960s Black Panther; Payless sneakers; Listerine and Camel cigarettes in his breath; thick beard; the hairline on the back of his neck a nappy cluster of Buddhaesque Bantu knots like black wool.

I have no shame about my dad's incarceration. I'm aware of how it can be deployed, though—I can shock certain elite (generally white) rooms with it, and I can use it as a form of code-switching, to signal a certain kind of affinity and shared experience in Black and brown rooms. I sometimes divulge his status as an incarcerated Black person—and my status as his daughter—to demonstrate that, though I have many trappings of privilege, I don't come from a purely privileged place. I know my dad made choices that put him in prison, and I also know that as a poor, big, Black man born in 1938, his options were few. Los Angeles and southern California were not the Deep South—but they were no utopia. When my dad was born, public spaces from fire stations to beaches, from bars to hotels, were segregated. Gangs of white Angelinos were bombing and setting fire to Black people's houses, burning crosses on their lawns. The so-called Zoot Suit Riots and the Second Great Migration were on deck. Redlining was rampant. In other words, our racial caste system meant his choices—the roads on which he could walk through life—were profoundly limited, the racism of the state cherry-picking his options, some decent and some bad and some awful, since his birth. No, since before his birth. The state had been pounding at his family for generations. His Black great-grandmother was killed by racist vigilantes operating in her Texas town as a quasi-police force, using violence to enforce de jure and de facto white supremacy. And a generation or two before her, the family line is bludgeoned and frayed by chattel slavery in antebellum Alabama and Louisiana. *And that is just what we know.* We can call chattel slavery the start; we can call life in Alabama, Louisiana, and then Texas the middle; we can call the state scrambling my dad and his sisters in and out of foster care and institutions the middle, too; and we can call, I guess, how my dad died the end. Because I connect how he died to how the state inserted itself into his life. But it isn't *really* the end; I have Black and brown cousins who are entangled with the state, unable to unwind its ropes from their limbs. I am spared from the state's grasp—by the strange alchemy of light skin and private school—and it's a cause for thanksgiving, even though I still contend with the caste system the state enforces. And I contend with how the state redacts us. Its violence becomes unbearable and we black it out. My dad didn't discuss Camarillo or prison. My aunts didn't discuss Camarillo or foster care until I asked them to. There are swaths of time and being that the state stole, blacked over. That are too traumatic to retell, hence my dad's "need-to-know" attitude. Within these redacted spaces—redactions in our lives—are countless unreported, unrecorded, unknowable indignities and harms that poured from the state onto my family's Black and brown generations, like tar. The state, the state—maker of slaves, trafficker of bodies, thief of children, grave of memories, grave of families, wicked and bigoted decider of fates, reaching forward and backward in time.

I think about my second-great-grandmother a lot these days. The one who was killed by racist vigilantes in the 1890s. These vigilantes were White Cappers, not members of the police but self-proclaimed law enforcement. Many of these white men took inspiration from antebellum slave patrols (the prototype of modern policing), and would eventually be absorbed into the Ku Klux Klan. In the intervening decades, White Cappers often harassed and killed Black people in pursuit of their crooked and racist—but utterly mainstream—notions of justice. My great-great-grandmother's name was Laura, and when I contemplate her last moments—the white-hooded men with dark guns in their hands, their footfalls on the porch—I think she must have known someone in her family was going to be hurt or killed. Or perhaps not, and this option might be worse—that the harassment of racist, self-styled law enforcement might be normal, and when she saw the White Cappers she merely braced herself for the drip-drip of more garden-variety persecution. The White Cappers believed (incorrectly) that Laura and her husband were harboring a Black vagrant. They demanded to enter the home and search it. But Laura's husband said no, and the White Cappers aimed and opened fire. A spray of their bullets moved through the open door and punctured Laura's visibly pregnant body. She tried to flee to another room and they shot her again. Her living children and her husband watched this shooting, and over the next hour, they watched her and the child in her womb die. The loop of this double murder plays itself around and around in my head: the ghoulish white masks of the killers, the smell of their gunshots, Laura's blood on the walls and the floor and the bed, the cries of her living children and husband. And the exhausting futility of distinguishing between sources of racist violence plays itself out, too: The White Cappers were not the state in the same way that, say, the Texas Rangers were, but they represented its norms and often acted in its name. If you're Black, you know that the line between the formal state and the informal state has always been porous. The "state" is a nebulous animal; sometimes its work is done by officials with titles and badges, and sometimes its work is done by rogue militias. The two can literally overlap. When it comes to preserving the most foundational law of this land—the so-called supremacy of white life and inferiority of Black and brown life—the state has two faces, one governmental and sunlit, the other an eminence grise, a gangster with shadowed, bloody hands. Both faces terrorize us. Both faces carry on, hammering at our humanity. Restitution is often elusive or impossible— grand juries don't indict; victims aren't believed; choices are circumscribed and shitty; lives are irreplaceable. Like a vast corporation, the state answers only to its shareholders and their appetites. Black people rarely own stock.

There is an obvious difference between my dad and my second-great-grandmother: she was innocent, he was guilty. He was always clear about having committed the crimes of which he was convicted, or if not those exact crimes, then similar crimes that had gone unseen. Laura's only "crime" was her existence. Still, I can't help seeing the state in how they both died. Laura, shot in her own home, is clear-cut. My dad's death was different, of natural causes—but also inseparable from the same racism that killed Laura, from how both deaths are connected to state power, whether exerted by its formal or would-be agents.

For the last twenty years of his life, my dad lived on a ranch where, instead of paying rent to the white couple who owned the property, he helped work and manage the land. His landlords called him the Big Nig. Six foot four, big-boned, Black. He laughed about it. And I laughed when he told me; that seemed to be the reaction he wanted. But it always bothered me, rankled me, made me want to spit in their faces. I was generally rude to them when I visited. Cold, icy; aware that my iciness probably didn't serve my dad, who relied (or chose to rely) on the economy he and the landlords had created.

His shack was down a dirt road, and had a bare cement floor and holes in the walls. The inside was dark, crowded, and dirty. Stacks of plastic bins, filled with his old court papers and photographs, lined the walls. Clothes and fly swatters hung from pipes across the ceiling. On makeshift shelves were pots and pans, big empty pickle jars, a basket of pill bottles for COPD, thousands of screws and nuts and bolts, and radios. My dad's sunken bed was in the middle of the room, dank with sweat-stained pillows the color of tea rings, and the Pendleton blanket my husband and I gave him, which was one of our wedding gifts but which we knew would better serve my dad in that windy, cold shack where he lived.

There were problems with the house in every season. December rain came under the door, March wind pried apart the wooden-slat walls, September heat pressed the roof down. The rodents loved it. There was no refrigerator. There was no water. There was no electricity, just a generator as needed and its grizzly hum, hooked up to the space heater or his breathing equipment. I tried to help him leave, or tried to try—in retrospect, my efforts were half-hearted because, though I felt guilt and shame that my dad lived that way, I was ambivalent about what it would take to help him. He had no money and could not hold a traditional job anymore, though, when I was a kid, he had managed to work periodically as a bakery's truck driver, or doing setup work for a caterer, or doing construction, and, as needed, selling drugs. The only way to improve his living situation toward the end of his life would have been to buy him a trailer, which he refused, or have him move in with us, which he refused, too. He was so deeply acclimated— institutionalized—to a decrepit domesticity, to something most people would call untenable or unhabitable, that it seemed likely he'd be more physically and psychologically comfortable in our basement than in a house. So we offered him that, as strange as it might sound and look to other people. But he was not interested in moving.

He wanted to stay where he was. Or he did not want to be anywhere else. It was solitary and peaceful. Its topography gave him a perch on which to sit, binoculars in hand, shoes in the golden California dirt, and watch the passersby on the far-off freeway. It was gorgeous and quiet, that flat brim of grassy land, with the gentle smell and sounds of far-off cows, and the shush of long grass blowing in the wind that rose each after- noon off the Pacific and poured over the hills, and a big sky, an unobstructed, Midwest kind of sky, that held his tiny house like an enormous, blue hand. I think it must have appealed to the part of him that ran away from home; the part of him that squatted on his haunches, toes near the edge of the boxcar, arms on his knees, blade of grass in his lips, watching America from the train tracks; the part of him that was a runaway kid becoming a pool shark in Los Angeles and hanging around the fire station in Brawley; the part of him that was a renegade; but most especially the part of him that hated but was acclimated to prison, a place that is the opposite of the expansive, cupped hand of sky where he died.

He was first incarcerated at seventeen, and left prison for the last time at about forty, a few years before I was born.

Prison shaped the rest of his life, molding his innate appreciation for nature and stillness into a deep (crippling?) need for solitude and space. It also severely limited the kinds of expectations, exchanges, and rules—what you might call norms of society—he could tolerate. It made him unable to sit with his back to the door. It made him, at times, hypervigilant; there would be a sound on the street—a car backfiring, a neighbor hollering briefly—and he'd startle, suddenly focused on the window or the door, no longer in the room with us. It made him less able to withstand the choppy emotional sways and eddies that sometimes comprise family life in a house. It made him shop for food at 2 a.m., when the grocery store was empty. It made it harder for him to hold down jobs, and therefore made it harder to pay rent.

So I understand why the one-room shack, alone on a big patch of land, rent free except for his physical labor, appealed to him. There, unlike in prison, he could be left alone, physically and emotionally distant from other people and their needs, whims, power trips, and pain. He could discover his own sense of time, his own rhythm, unlike in prison. He was wrapped in nature—ladybugs and rabbits, vegetable gardens and citrus trees, dirt and dust, puddles and creeks, grass, wind, moonlight, daylight, and the sky—unlike in prison. His favorite thing to do was "set"—meaning, sit and watch the peace of his sweet corner. I'd call him and say, "Whatcha doin', Pops?" And he'd answer, "Oh, I'm just settin' here, watching the wind."

He must have known that the solitude of that place meant he might die alone, and perhaps slowly, if he had a bad fall or accident when his landlords were not around. He knowingly traded the safety and normalcy most of us rely on for a kind of freedom he'd never had. Even if his life compelled him to make that trade, he was, ultimately, at peace with it. And he did die alone.

I come back to what the coroner said: *It was quick, almost certainly quick.* In the early months, when my mind would frequently drop into a grisly, insane-making montage of him suffering alone and near death for days, this assurance pulled me back into myself, stopped the spinning. It reminded me of when I was an anxious kid, legs shaking as I tried to climb something, and how my dad would spot me and say, with warm certainty, "You're not gonna fall." I'd repeat it to myself: *it was quick, it was quick.* Maybe a brain hemorrhage or heart attack. But within days, or even hours, or possibly even minutes of getting the news, I remember asking myself whether it wasn't racism, slow and steady, that killed him. Whether but for its insistent grip on his shoulders, but for being trapped in its wake, he might have had a better death, let alone life.

Because here's what happened: his maroon truck, ramshackle but running, hadn't moved in days. Strange, because nearly every morning of his life he drove that truck across the property to check the land. And he was not answering his cell phone, though it was always—always—clipped to the neck of his T-shirt. And he was eighty years old, with diabetes and congestive heart failure and chronic obstructive pulmonary disorder. His landlords—inventors of that nickname, the Big Nig—knew all of this. They knew his health status, they knew his truck hadn't moved, and they knew he wasn't answering his phone, because they'd seen the truck stationary all week, and they'd tried calling him, too. After three days, they sent their son down to my dad's shack; the son observed that the door wasn't locked, but he didn't open it. He called, "Lee?" and hearing nothing, left. That was it. Three days later, the landlord's wife finally called my mom to say, "I think something might be wrong with Lee." She explained that he hadn't answered his phone or moved his truck in a week, and his door had been unlocked for days. The landlady said, "Do you think I should check on him?" And my mom hollered, "Yes!" The landlady said, "But I'm scared!" (Of what? Of his body—large and Black and male—even in death?) The landlady refused. I cannot separate any of this from how they called him the Big Nig. My mom drove to the ranch, opened the shack door, and saw his body. The coroner said he'd died six days before, and it was quick, almost certainly quick.

The continuity is haunting, and so very, very American. Alabama and Louisiana, where our tall, big-boned genes survived despite being treated like n*****s; a slurry of horrors unknown and unaccounted for through chattel slavery, Reconstruction, and Jim Crow; the White Cappers killing Laura and her unborn brown child in her home; my dad's father in and out of prison; the social worker Ms. Hall and her judgments; my dad in and out of foster care, of institutions, of prisons; the effects of prison—what we'd now probably call post-traumatic stress disorder; my dad's decision, both willing and forced, to live as he did, alone, isolated, paying rent with his body; his landlords accepting this unusual, funky situation and calling him, with a laugh, the Big Nig. He must have heard that, in some form or another, his whole life. Recently, I opened one of the storage crates we cleared out of his house to read his court papers. Trial transcripts, parole papers, letters to and from his family. In one transcript he is described, over and over, by every single witness, as the large Negro man. They pointed to him at the defense table and said, "The large Negro man sitting over there." Or described the guy with the gun, scooping jewelry from the case into a sack, as "a large Negro man, like him." Arrested, tried, convicted, prison; the state, the state; he made choices that set the state in motion, but how many choices did he actually have?

As a child, I wanted my dad to be angry about how racism had screwed him over. I wanted him to resent and rage against the power of the state, its immovable presence. But he would laugh, or sigh, and say, *You carry too much of the world on your shoulders, girl.* He may have just been, in the quiet season of his life, able to reflect on the world with equanimity. Still, when I became a lawyer, he cried and took my hands and said I was going to make people whole.

I have utterly failed to do this. I haven't lived up to his dream of righting wrongs, or forcing the state to cough up penance and amends. I don't think I've healed anyone's wounds, except maybe, partially, his. Nor can I—not when the system that harms us is so colossal and nimble, so all-seeing and powerful; I'm one person. What I wish I could tell him is that the wholeness *I* seek cannot be attained—not when the state hovers in the doorway, not when the state redacts decades and lifetimes, as if we never existed, or as if our existence were a mistake to be corrected. Instead of memories, we have gaps. Instead of memories that can be shared and tilled like soil, made to bring forth new beauty and knowledge—seventeen years of memories, in my dad's case—we have the state, with its vault and blade and black marker. We have, instead of overflowing, voluminous, unabridged lives, an extraordinary erasure. That cannot be made whole.

Nearly, Not Quite

I was a delightful candidate, different from the other women: a straight-A student at New York University, fluent in Italian, conversant in high-toned stuff like exhibitions at the Met and the latest *New Yorker*, and carrying a small Gucci purse to the interview; they hired me on the spot. The agency was called Town and Country. From a generic office in midtown Manhattan, a group of women with Long Island accents helped wealthy families find childcare for their bifurcated lives, weeks in the city and weekends in the country. I nannied for three families as I finished college. One job ended amicably because I graduated and moved, one tersely because I declined to spend my Christmas holiday working for them, and one family stopped calling after I told them their daughter seemed, in my view, to be reporting an incident of molestation through her make-believe play. It was a lonely job, spending days, nights, and weekends keeping uber-rich kids out of their parents' hair. Each dad worked on Wall Street. On weeknights, they'd slip into their families' infinite apartments after 10 p.m., passing through the kids' rooms to tousle hair and pull up blankets. On Fridays, the dads helicoptered from downtown Manhattan to the Hamptons to join their families, and I took the same trip on the Hampton Jitney. I stepped off the bus and saw the Suburban or Hummer waiting, sometimes driven by the mom and sometimes by a driver. I'd climb into the back and greet the kids with showy excitement, and we'd head for the helipad to get the dad, who would be harried and ticked off and communing with his BlackBerry. I envied the moms for marrying such consummately successful men, and I sneered at the men for their bare-minimum parenthood, which they seemed to justify with their paychecks. The moms were nice enough—not kind, but not rude. They were thin and pretty, but not great beauties. They were a pretty that is mostly about unlimited access to improvements and maintenance—dermatologists, surgeons, colorists, trainers. When I was alone in the houses, I'd walk to the master bedrooms and flip through the moms' bedside stacks of *Vogue* and *Harper's Bazaar,* lusting in my fingertips and throat after what they could put on their bodies, and jealous of their bodies, too, which were worthy of such finery: Agent Provocateur and La Perla, Clé de Peau Beauté and Frédéric Fekkai, Bliss lemon-sage cream from the actual Bliss salon, Mario Badescu before it was in every coed's medicine cabinet, Ferragamo shoes that were tiny regardless of size, and Oscar de la Renta gowns thick with architecture. It seemed profoundly unfair that I could appreciate these trappings of money, that I understood intuitively how these rich splendors could be medicinal to your body, but that voyeurism was as close as I'd get to experiencing it myself. Sometimes I'd be asked to run an errand, and I'd drive the shining, heavy cars myself, buying groceries at Cavaniola's or picking up the mom's new Jack

Rogers sandals, pretending I was living my own life, pretending onlookers saw me not as who I was, but as who I *almost* was, who I had the potential to be.

Most of these families had two or three nannies. We were fungible to them, but by having more than one they inadvertently turned us into allies. Our numbers gave us a ballast in the house that we wouldn't have otherwise had. At the picnic table, at the country club, there might be four of them—the family members—but also four of us. I wonder if they ever felt effectively outnumbered by the collective heft of our Black and brown presence, or knew that we often felt superior to them despite our low status. My relationship with Nia, a baby nanny from Trinidad with a child of her own, comes to mind. I was in charge of the older kids while Nia tended to our employer's three-month-old, keeping her quiet, comfortable, and out of sight. She and the baby shared a room, a small nursery that was as far from the master bedroom as was possible in the layout of that house. This family loved hosting parties on Friday and Saturday nights, and there was always a half hour after dinner, when the fireflies were out and the kids hung around the adults, that I took a break, though we didn't call it that. I'd relax by standing alone in the kitchen, scarfing something sweet and carby and listening for the footsteps of my employer or their guests, ready to turn it back on if needed. Then I'd walk to the nursery to check out the evening's pajamas. Every night after dinner, Nia dressed the baby in an elaborate, dainty, white sleeping outfit. She mixed and matched tops and bottoms in different ways, sometimes adding a ribbon around the baby's freshly bathed head. I'd stand in the doorway and watch as Nia lay on her side on the twin bed, beside the baby and a stack of options, holding little garments to her small body and saying, "Nah," or "Yes, this is the one Mommy will like!" When the baby was dressed, Nia would freshen her makeup, smooth her white uniform, moisturize her hands, and carry the decked-out baby around the room for the parents and their guests, pausing to hold her out like a photograph. After the oohs and ahhs, Nia and the baby retreated to the nursery and Nia put her down for the night. I don't doubt that these parents loved their children, including their youngest daughter; but aside from the occasional peek into the crib or passing tickle on the belly, these evening parades are the only occasions on which I remember our employers spending time with their baby.

Late at night, alone in the kitchen, Nia and I would pour ourselves glasses of water and sit at the long, shining table to rehash the day and its familiar patterns. Sometimes Nia would finally eat her dinner, usually take-out leftovers she heated in the microwave. (That kitchen was a marvel—massive, all white, with two refrigerators and two sinks, and tended by a housekeeper morning, noon, and night; I saw her drying the sinks with a cotton rag all day, whenever someone got water, so that the sinks were almost always immaculate, seemingly unused. Watching this housekeeper, I had an epiphany: rich people aren't cleaner or more careful or more organized than the rest of us—they just pay people to clean up after them and continually grease the wheels.) Whispering, Nia and I dissected the brief, polite nightly viewing of the baby, found it bizarre and cold. We chuckled at the mom, who slowly cut herself exact, precise halves of breakfast muffins to stave off calories.

We rolled our eyes at the dad, who fancied himself such a big important man but didn't know how much of his life was handed to him. Occasionally, we gossiped with relief about moments in which we witnessed the family's humanity and love for one another. How the mom had a nickname for the new baby that she said in a goofy voice. Or how, when a car sped through the crosswalk, narrowly missing the dad and his six-year-old daughter, he swooped his child up and bellowed, "Hey! My kid's here!" And we relived their presumptuousness—how, for example, I'd been volunteered to babysit over a dozen children I'd never met for the families gathered at a retired golf star's last-minute barbecue.

Still, I was always torn about who I should express more allegiance to—the white people who employed me, or the brown women with whom I shared my role. I felt a physical closeness and a sense of common cause with the other caregivers, but also a persistent, uncomfortable apartness, too. We were all brown, and mostly black-brown. We all slept on thin mattresses in tiny rooms near the service elevators or back doors. We were all given twenty-dollar CVS gift cards so we could leave a set of drugstore toiletries at the country house instead of schlepping them each week. In New York City, we spent the same weeknights supervising homework and making cups of tea for our charges, brushing tiny teeth and reading bedtime books as city life unfolded beyond the bunkeresque apartment walls. In the Hamptons, we white-knuckled the same isolated, taxing weekends, carrying bowls of Pirate's Booty down hydrangea-lined paths to the pool, or jogging to pick up tennis balls from the far half of the court, or wiping pink butts and holding our expressions still against the repellent stench of someone else's shit. These shared indignities—which were racialized by our circumstances—bonded us. But I was light-skinned, and this granted me a privilege. I was culturally whiter, too. I had natural nails and theirs were acrylic. I spoke private school English and they didn't—theirs was laced with West Indian inflections and the cadence of Black English. I wore my hair natural and they wore weaves. I was a young college student and this job was a means to an end, while they were older and the job seemed like a career. I was childless, while they had to outsource their mothering to grandmas and friends during the enervating weeklong shifts. When we all sat at the dinner table—nannies, kids, and parents—I was unsure which side I was on. I understood the dad's erudite references to things like Adam Smith and Milton Friedman, and I knew what he was communicating—though I didn't agree with it—when he called the *New York Times* "that communist rag." I knew what the moms meant when they debated barre methods and pondered going "Bergdorf blonde." I could picture the paintings they loved at the Met because I'd seen them, too. I, too, had a bottle of Chanel perfume on my dresser. That I shouldn't make much of this I somehow intuited. My employers did not want kinship with their employee. A (brown) nanny who could quote Walt Whitman and took her *own* barre classes would trouble the seamlessness of our arrangement, and I wanted their unfettered approval. I also wanted to preserve my closeness with the other staff, the nannies, housekeepers, gardeners, and house managers who were my commiserating comrades in the delicately balanced ecosystem of those six-bedroom apartments high above Fifth, Madison, and Park Avenues, in the ocean-side mansions of our Long Island weekends.

Sitting at those Upper East Side and Bridgehampton dinner tables reminded me of the anxiety and loneliness that I felt in first grade when, as I played alone on a branch of the tree in the schoolyard, the Black girls in the class approached me. I remember them as dark-skinned, with hair parted into puffs and braids, tied back with pom-pom elastics. They weren't rich. The kids of color arrived by bus from neighborhoods with less access. One girl said to me, "You Black?" I don't remember my answer, though I remember the foggy, menacing confusion I felt. Whatever I said, she answered, "But you know you Black, right?" The other Black girls agreed; then they left me on the tree, alone and pudgy in my grown-up-sized jacket. If I was Black, like them, then why did they leave?

Many years later, while alone on vacation in Palm Springs, I thought about these memories and conundrums—of being like but unlike the nannies, like but unlike my privileged employers, like but unlike the girls at school. I was alone because I wasn't dating anyone, and my friends from law school were all celebrating spring break taking exotic trips I couldn't yet afford. Maybe I'd also, someday, have the means to visit Tokyo, Paris, and London for quick getaways, too; but not while I was living on student loans. Not until I graduated from law school and began my job at a law firm where I'd be making a starting salary of close to $180,000 a year. I pondered living decisively within my means and spending spring break walking around Oakland's Lake Merritt, sunbathing on my balcony, organizing my closets. But that felt too depressing, so I found a flight-and-ritzy-hotel package and put it on my credit card.

It wasn't a fun vacation. The resort was crammed with couples, and I was so self-conscious about being alone that I forced myself to stay busy instead of rest. I walked three miles to buy a date milkshake from a too-cold creamery that smelled like bleach and I had heartburn for hours. I wandered downtown and overpaid for a bad pedicure. I popped into the Trina Turk boutique and ran my fingertips along the popsicle-bright clothes, all too expensive and too small for me, but pretended the shopgirls didn't know that. I saw bland exhibits in local galleries. In my hotel room, I took selfies in the bathroom mirror wearing my bikini, aping supermodel poses and trying to hold my phone at an angle that suggested someone else took the pictures.

My sense of solitude was sharpened by a familiar sense of uncertainty. There were brown people at the resort, like me. And there where white people there, too. But I wasn't at home with either group.

The brown people I saw weren't tourists, there to spend money and relax—they were Spanish-speaking waitresses, housekeepers, and gardeners who moved constantly around the resort in their uniforms and sensible shoes, serving wine to high-paying guests, stripping used bedsheets, grooming azalea bushes. When I left the resort to walk through town, the brown people I saw were Spanish speakers dressed for yard work and milling in clusters on the sidewalk, or crowded into the kitchens of every restaurant, flipping pancakes and drizzling sauce from squeeze bottles. They were not at galleries or getting pedicures or considering the offerings at the Trina Turk store.

I adore, even crave, fancy hotels and resorts, and I don't generally vacation unless I can afford such accommodations. (Don't judge me, I've earned this.) Yet I'm always awkward and uncomfortable being served by a brown person, and it's almost always brown people doing the serving. Our culture's idea of service is so racialized it's nearly ritualistic; I can't recall the last time I encountered a white woman giving an Asian woman a pedicure, or a white woman cleaning a Latina's house. Under our norms, me *being served* instead of serving feels like a breach. The whole time my nails are being painted or my lunch is being walked over, I want to exchange knowing looks with hotel staff about the blithe privilege of the white guests. I want to explain that while I am technically one of the guests, I don't really fit in with that group. But class does count for something, and I'm not sure the staff would see it my way.

When you vacation alone, you watch people. There was a white couple staying at that same Palm Springs resort and I could not take my eyes off them. They showed up at the pool just after me, and they were unmistakably—almost palpably—rich. I could tell by their clothes and jewelry, but mostly by the calm confidence that hovered around their bodies. He wore long swim shorts and Havaianas flip-flops, JFK sunglasses resting atop his kicky brown haircut. She wore white linen pants and a

Burberry shawl wrapped tight around her thin torso despite the heat, and her face seemed artfully Botoxed. The man sipped his drink, reclining on one elbow, his barrel chest hairy and tan, his belly soft and irreverent. The woman dropped the shawl, pulled off the white tank top beneath, and untied the waist of her pants. The pants fell in a soft puddle at her maroon-lacquered toes. Her body was lean and taut like wicker, her pale skin spotted with freckles like cinnamon shook over milk. She was naked except for a Burberry string bikini. I wondered whether her breasts were real. She sipped her drink, then reclined beside him and removed a Kindle from her straw bag. They sat in silence, she reading, him gazing across the patio and pool, though his dark sunglasses concealed where his gaze fell.

They were precisely the kind of couple I nannied for. But here, at this resort, we were on something closer to equal footing. We were all guests. We were all adults. I wasn't being paid to take care of their children. To the contrary: I was about to graduate from one of the country's best law schools and join one of the country's most elite law firms, making hundreds of thousands of dollars to defend naughty corporations and their executives. And with those hundreds of thousands, I would be able to afford clothes from Saks and furniture from Restoration Hardware and rides in the back of town cars. I was, in other words, about to look the part, and maybe even *be* the part. And I wanted the white couple to see it, maybe because my employers had not—how alike we were, how much our sensibilities overlapped, that I was their peer and equal now, and maybe always had been. (It only dawned on me later that equals don't need validation.) I wanted to please them. Them with their money and grooming, their certainty that they deserved their good lot in life. I tried to resist it, the itch to get into their aura. The itch left me squirming inside. After all, I knew they were the sort of people who'd assume I worked at a store when I was actually shopping there; who'd cross the street to avoid walking beside my large, dark-skinned dad but who could never imagine themselves doing these things. Still, I felt like a dog who smelled a treat in their pockets, the treat of their very existence.

They were in the hot tub when I had my first chance to yoke myself to them. His vibe was the same as it had been that morning, half languid hedonism and half hearty gusto; and she was still orderly, sitting in a tight way that kept her breasts above the water, as if they'd dissolve when wet. Post-dunk water streamed down his face, hers was dry.

I stepped into the tub, aware that I hadn't totally shaved my bikini line and wondering if they could see, and suddenly aware of the frizz in my ponytail. My eagerness to prove myself was overwhelming.

She didn't look over as I settled in the water, but he did. "Hi," he said gamely.

"Hi," I replied.

She launched into a monologue about her gold bracelet. The speech was directed solely to him. It was difficult to find, she said, because of the market for that type of vintage. She then described how and why she'd gone off silver ages ago. Without responding to her, he changed the subject. He said, "Have you noticed how that gardener is an *exact* replica of Jeff

Bridges?" She cried, "Yes!" and slid off her perch so her breasts were now submerged. (They didn't dissolve, though they did seem, in their perfection, like the sugar-lump miracles Picasso talked about. "Everything is a miracle. It is a miracle that one does not dissolve in one's bath like a lump of sugar.")

"And he's working it," he continued. "He could style himself differently, but he doesn't." She nodded and removed her hand from the water, adjusting her bracelet and submerging it again. She said, "I bet he can go into any restaurant in LA and say 'Table for Bridges.'"

I knew who they were discussing—the head gardener was the only white staff person I saw aside from the front desk crew. I decided to go for it. "I'm sorry to interject, but have you heard him *speak*?"

The man turned to me. "Yes! The voice is identical. You know I've heard Jeff Bridges is a method actor. Maybe it's him."

"Anything is possible," I said, and turned casually away as if to realign my back with a jet, but really it was to return the conversation to them exclusively. I smiled to myself. I'd made a connection.

When they got out of the water, she didn't say goodbye. I don't remember if he did. Could she have been jealous of a random chick chatting up her husband? Or was I just beneath her and invisible, with my frayed Target suit and wacky hair and back fat and chipped nails? Her slight, tiny as it was, did not feel random. I remembered the girls from first grade. I remembered the nannies and the rich families, how the nannies would laugh when I didn't get a Black cultural reference and the rich families would scoff when I proposed a higher rate for working on holidays. It was déjà vu—being reduced to what you represent to someone else instead of being seen for what you are.

I watched the white couple the whole weekend. I imagined the me I'd have to be to actually connect with them, and the daydream got elaborate. This me was still Black, but she was born rich and was what you might call bougie. If she was mixed, she was a different kind of mixed—not the "whole lot of yellow wasted" that I've been called—more like Halle Berry. Brown skin, white features. She would have chatted easily with the white husband and wife because they were of the same economic cloth and, being born rich, she knew it. They would know it, too—skin color notwithstanding, the firm tone of her body and classiness of her maillot and armor-like gleam of her nude manicure, the crispness of her straightened bob and the tidiness of her pool bag and the cute fit of her straw hat would have signaled to them, *We're alike.* The white wife would love me; throwing her head back, she'd exclaim, "Oh my god, you're so funny!" Or, "I know, right?" agreeing happily with something I'd opined. We'd all have dinner—it would be the wife's idea. She'd suddenly say, "Oh my god, let's all go to *Barco* for dinner!" and glance quickly at her husband, touching his arm to get his assent, her eyes bright and happy, and he'd say, "Sure, let's do it, I'll make a res," and I would say, "Oh, that would be fun!" We'd leave the resort in separate cars, and there might be a brief, under-the-breath comment from my husband about having to spend the whole night with these white people. My husband would be Black, like me, and well-heeled and well-educated and worldly, too, but less eager to please the white duo. Maybe because he was a man and pleasing people mattered less to him in general. At the restaurant, the fictional Barco: three bottles of wine, bits of ribeye and salmon left on the plates, one slice of flourless cake split four ways with four tiny spoons, the waitress rolling her eyes in the kitchen, two coffees and one tea and one hot water with lemon, the men to the sidewalk so the white husband could have his cigar. Us women would stay at the table, our maxi dresses like hibiscus flowers pressed against our tans, our Tory Burch wedges tiny and pert under the table. The white wife would be drunk and convivial, very buddy-buddy. I would be tipsy but watchful—there would have been some incident, some moment when, despite how alike we all were, the white couple's whiteness would have irked or grated on us. Maybe this: maybe my husband had squeezed my hand hard as if to say *Get me out of here* during what we'd later call "the Ebonics incident." Here's what happened: the white husband was a filmmaker, it turns out, and keen to tell us about his new documentary. He described filming Black kids playing basketball at a city court. And as he described the beautiful melee they made, the bright thwack of the bouncing ball, the shadow-making of their loping legs and swinging arms, he mimicked how they spoke to each other, these inner-city kids, and we chafed at the sound of Black English coming from his mouth, again and again, as if there was nothing about this overstepping, awkward display that should make him feel self-conscious.

There's something peculiar about this fantasy, which I turned around and around in my head all weekend at that hotel: I'm not me, as if I'm not worthy of my own daydreams. Indeed, I inverted myself. Instead of being an ambiguous, light-skinned, Black-featured, strange kind of pretty, I clarified my looks: medium-dark skin, white features, straight hair—a Eurocentric-pretty kind of Black. I erased my visual ambiguity. I erased my class ambiguity, too. In real life, I have worked my way into money—but I still remember markers of deprivation. The pinching repetition of being teased for my Payless shoes and lame clothes, and the shame of my dad's house, which had plastic sheets over holes in the roof and a bucket in which we went to the bathroom because there was no running water or functional toilet. In the daydream, this friction and ambiguity are gone. I'm born rich, or close enough to rich that becoming rich is a seamless transition. And instead of being chronically single and afraid of spinsterhood, I'm married—in other words: clearly, publicly, and permanently chosen. Wanted and claimed. I am wrapped in acceptance.

My second chance to get in with the white couple was so brief and spastic it hardly counts. I sat on a poolside bench drinking wine in my hotel robe. The robe was a little snug. The wine was lovely. All weekend—as usual—I'd tried to signal my sense of embarrassment and solidarity to the brown waiters by making friendly eye contact and asking how their day was, if they had weekend plans. This guy I thanked twice—one hearty thanks when he set the glass down, and a chipper "Thanks, again!" as he walked away. Over the top, maybe, but I felt I was correcting for how often other guests didn't even acknowledge the staff, as if bots and androids were creating their heavenly, upscale experience, not people. (It was also, I'm aware, the kind of performative, give-me-a-break behavior I might see in a white guest and roll my eyes at, like, *If you want to be kind to the hoi polloi, spend money at a nonprofit, not a fucking resort.*)

My reading glasses and a Lincoln biography sat on the bench next to my thigh. Along came Husband, with his shirtless walk proclaiming middle-aged pride, and the Wayfarers, again perched on his head, hooting endless youth.

He stopped short, eyes near my leg, and said, "How's that book?"

I looked down. The book was *Team of Rivals*, and I thought to myself, *Like my brain*, where my identities vie for prominence. I said, "Fantastic. Are you a history buff?"

"Big time. I've been eyeing it."

"You should definitely get it." I paused. I should have left well enough alone. But no. I added, "And the price is right—two bucks used on Amazon."

He raised his eyebrows like, *Imagine that!* "Well," he said, "I guess you can't beat that."

I immediately wished I could unsay my fiscal epilogue—though it would occur to the hotel staff to buy used books to save money, it would never occur to him. Betwixt and between, despite my efforts.

The next day, the husband and wife weren't at the pool. I noticed their absence. I almost missed them—they'd given me something to do besides obsess about my solitude. They'd given me a Rubik's Cube to fiddle with—could I make them see and like me as a peer? Could I curry favor not only with them, but their kind of future? I wondered if I'd made an impression on either of them. Maybe, lying in bed, he'd said to her, "That girl from the hot tub was nice, huh?" And she'd roll closer to him, teasingly say, "Oh? She caught your eye, did she?" Or maybe, strolling to the restaurant, she'd say, "That girl from the hot tub had gorgeous hair." And he'd say, "What made you think of that?" And she'd shrug and say, "I just noticed her, I guess." More likely, I was interchangeable to them— just The Black Woman, someone filling a slot that any Black woman could fill, like at work when I'm called by the other Black women's names and I'm suddenly even more invisible, even more alone.

I imagined the brown hotel housekeepers entering their now-empty suite, witnessing the detritus of their stay—a chocolate bar wrapper in the trash, a half-empty bottle of expensive water. I imagined the couple with their lightly packed stuff, a few luxurious T-shirts and swimsuits and sweaters in their leather weekend bags, magazines and gadgets in the side pockets, getting into a spotless car and driving west, toward Los Angeles. I imagined them thinking about the future, and seeing themselves in it. I imagined them relaxed, restored, not really talking, which might make them wonder about whether they were happy. Maybe they weren't. But they knew who they were. They knew where they belonged, tucked deep in the shelter of a fixed category, together.

I compare that to my perpetual, prismatic, in-betweenness around race and class—I am the person whose brown dad had plywood nailed over the drafty holes where window panes should've been, the wind perpetually thinning the warmth from the lone propane tank heater; and I'm also the person who has walked through the West Wing of the White House, who attended sixteen years of private (white) school, who became an attorney. Don't get me wrong: there's freedom and power in the liminal spaces, freedom and power I don't want to give up—with a subtle turn of the dial I can shape-shift, I can sync myself to you. I can create rapport, I can mirror, I can be like any of the parts of myself, inhabiting any piece of myself fully enough to "belong" to the racial or class group in which I happen to find myself. Still, it is often a companionless place. I have sometimes looked at people like the rich, white couple at the hotel, and my former employers, and, even though it's more complicated, the Black and brown nannies and housekeepers, and eyed their camaraderie and "fixedness" with jealousy. Sometimes I would prefer a life in which no adjustment was necessary, in which many people were like me. Sometimes I'd prefer an easy fit.

On the Sources of
Cultural Identity

I picked Italy because I was studying Western art, and NYU
had a villa in a hilly olive orchard in Tuscany. I also picked
Italy because, as I stared at the poster tacked to a corkboard
in the study abroad office, I remembered, with a sting, years
before: the dark Manhattan living room of some rich friends
from high school (cloth tartan wallpaper, heavy silk curtains,
and a gaggle of Cavalier King Charles spaniels silent in their
crates), sitting akimbo on the floor like kindergarteners as we
smoked and ate potato chips and watched the 1999 remake of
The Talented Mr. Ripley, a film that takes place in a lusciously
stylized 1950s Italy. They continually paused it to compare
notes, with gusto and pleasure, about their visits to the Spanish Steps and the Amalfi Coast, their suites at the St. Regis
on Via Vittorio. I stared out the windows at silent, bustling
Madison Avenue below us; having never been to Europe, let
alone for an expensive vacation, I had nothing to add to these
bursts of memory. In the jazz club scene, my friends joined
the actors in the chorus of *Tu Vuò Fà L'Americano*—a song that

pokes swinging fun at an Italian's blundering attempts to seem American—bopping their heads and waving their arms, blissful at the sound of their own Italian singing. I was bitterly conscious of my invisibility, and mesmerized by the apparent expansiveness of their worlds compared to mine.

Italy was a good choice for me because I absolutely, whole-hog, madly, truly adored it.

I arrived in Florence for a year's study gauzy with jetlag and wordless except for *cappuccino* and *ciao*, smiling like a drunk as I toddled down the pebbled path to my host family. Within a week I felt at home among the curving cobbled streets and smoky cafes, the musical loops and rhythms of the language. I picked up Italian with preternatural speed. Learning and speaking it gave me conspicuous, almost embarrassing joy. I felt musical and buzzed, a little wild, very free. I learned vocabulary and grammar like *that*, jumped two levels in class before the end of the year. My accent was thrillingly good, nearly perfect. I ate in far-off restaurants where you didn't see Americans or hear English, and relished learning new phrases from waiters. I learned slang. I spoke aloud to myself around the house. I watched Italian movies, listened to Ligabue and Giorgia CDs, copied Italian newspapers into my journal. I understood why my New York high school friends were transformed into flirty, neon versions of their best selves while singing along to *tu vuò fà l'Americano, l'Americano, l'Americano*. And my own fluency, which quickly surpassed theirs, was transporting in deeper ways, too: speaking Italian so well let me *feel* Italian, and feeling Italian meant *not* feeling American. Which is to say, suddenly removed from America's insistence on reminding people of color of their coloredness, I experienced racelessness in the way I imagine white people often do. It was a remarkable—and fleeting—liberation.

Fueled by my fluency and a real—if temporary—sense of self-determination, most of my Italian memories are terrific: I eagerly embraced the local look, throwing out my American wardrobe and spending my cotton-soft lire on clothes from Miss Sixty, Benetton, and Diesel. I did my eyeliner like the Italian girls, heavy, black, and swooping. I wore Dolce & Gabbana Light Blue perfume. Modeling Italians, I swore off cappuccini after morning. I grinned at the buoyant freedom of eating pizza Italian style—an entire pie per person. I got myself a cute Florentine boyfriend with curly blond hair and blue Superga sneakers, and we drove his old Porsche to Castiglioncello, his big, rough hand resting lax on the stick shift. We stayed in a yellow house near Marcello Mastroianni's place, watching Italian vacationers dip in the cool Ligurian Sea, their tan bodies shining like brass in the August sun. On Capri, my girlfriends and I took taxis to Marina Piccola. We ate cheese, tomatoes, and bread, and we drank chianti. We catnapped in black bathing suits; daydreamed of swimming, slick as dolphins, to the yachts harbored in the turquoise water; rolled onto our sides to watch guys roughhousing in the waves; and walked in flip-flops with beach-heavy, relaxed legs up the long steps to Chiesa di Sant'Andrea, a white breadbox of a church, to imagine our wedding days. In Rome, I felt allied to the ruins, as if among kin, while I crossed the same flat stones as Caesar and the Vestal Virgins. I ate an achingly delicious wedge of lasagna at a hole in the wall near the Vatican. At Christmastime, I popped roasted chestnuts into my mouth and sat alone in the crisp evening air near the Trevi Fountain, listening to the Americans and Germans, smug about how to the manner born I was, and the fact that my emotional allegiance was to Italy. I took the bus to the Villa Borghese and spent afternoons there, a thick white book of Italian grammar and copy of *Grazia* in my tan suede bag, and never tired of circling Bernini's *Apollo and Daphne*, with Daphne's mouth soft and open like half a white peach and the inferno of stone leaves overtaking her fingertips. Same thing, *The Rape of Proserpina*, with her marble thigh warm and doughy, the tender underside of her feet almost caught in Cerberus's bite, and Pluto's fingers full of shadow so that they look dirty, the knuckles and cuticles black as the fingers of a mechanic. I savored the overlap between daily life and the ancient: how I passed Michelangelo Buonarroti's childhood home while walking to the gym, how Dante might have lingered on the same bench where I read the paper and ate strawberry gelato at sunset.

This bounding glee, my jubilant, carefree absorption of Italy and my enmeshment with the culture was so euphoric that it could not last. A weekend in France reminded me who I was, and of the limitations race imposes on us even when we briefly forget them.

Ready for a foray into another country, my roommates and I boarded a silver train at Florence's main station and felt like sophisticates as it raced northwest, blue passports and a little worldliness in our hands. From vinyl seats we looked through scratched-up windows out to the horizon. After a moment, my roommates dropped their eyes to their books but I continued watching Italy. Seeing the chalky hillsides and the crystalline cubes of distant marble quarries, I imagined Michelangelo, on whom I had an art-student crush, just over the hillcrest with his leather belt of chisels. I watched the ocean appear and disappear, and imagined that the yachts lined up like piano keys were a good omen—a promise of a stylish, lucky future. I memorized little cardboard-cutout train stations and the shape and color of the clothes hung to dry between apartments. I watched the coiffed, chic adults with sweaters tied gently over their shoulders as they strolled; bowlegged old men in hats; old women in long plain skirts; Italian teenagers with ratty, flared jeans and topknots, nose rings and throaty laughs to match their cigarettes; Italian guys hopping on Vespas, one's slim arms around the other's slim waist, both leaning into an accelerating curve. I wanted to merge with all of it. I wanted to become Italian; to shed the America that seemed to stand between where I happened to be born and who I actually was. Italy felt like *the real universe* the way Manhattan does when you first arrive.

Our train pulled into Gare de Nice-Ville and we stepped into the chilly French air. "Hello, France!" we called out. I remember being refreshed by Nice's new foreignness. For breakfast, we ate scrambled eggs as silky as custard and milky coffees served in big bowls. We sensed a hedonism in France that would have been frowned upon in Florence, and, being twenty, decided to each buy a bottle of red wine and drink it, topless, at the beach. The ocean was uninviting on an overcast October day but, once drunk, we waded in happily, our feet wobbling on rocks and the seawater leaving a patina of French salt on our calves. Our cheap hotel room was on a courtyard and kitty-corner from windows of a family's apartment. At night, the window shone gold from the lights within, and we listened to the sounds of their big dinners, pondering whether the husky French words were more beautiful than Italian.

What struck me like a gong that weekend, though, was the presence of brown-skinned people—more in one walk to the beach than I'd seen in two months in Florence—and how segregated they seemed from white French life. It reminded me, *Oh yeah, race is a thing*. And, *I'm Black*. To be sure, seeing Black people made Nice feel more like America in good ways. Nice became, through the presence of a Black population, a diverse city that was part of our shared globe, not just its own world. But, also like America, I could sense and see that Nice was a place where *blackness* meant something suspect, where it existed at a remove from "normal" or "true" French life. These Black and brown Niçois were mostly Africans. They stood in skinny clusters, dressed in tracksuits, bald-headed and smoking at bars where soccer matches were played on high-mounted televisions. They sat on folding chairs in Internet cafes, legs jangling, and chattered a carbonated seltzery mix of French and African tongue into little black flip phones. They walked with bags of groceries on each hip toward whatever lay outside the city center, their hair wrapped in cloth. They did not, as far as I saw, hang out with white French people in public. I struggled with their presence in my own way. On the one hand, simply having Black people around made me less of a visual oddity and helped me feel acclimated on some instant, preverbal level. On the other hand, these French Africans were so incredibly foreign to me, foreign within foreign like double hearsay, that I couldn't actually relate to them at all. They were a mystery. I couldn't imagine their inner lives and moment-to-moment reactions to life the way I can when I share culture and history with people. And if they felt any affinity for me, they didn't show it. I thank France for teaching me the tragic lesson that *African American* and *African* are not alike. I had seen Africans before, but seeing them in a new environment, far from my home, clarified our differences. This lesson may not be tragic to Africans (or West Africans, to be more precise), but it is to this Black American—a person who is almost by definition searching for a home. We share a root with each other, a common genetic and cultural lineage, but after the ordeal of American centuries, our offshoot is almost wholly distinct from the original seed. So distinct that we are, in fact, almost rootless. I resisted, but had to accept, the news that my brethren and I were not close anymore.

By contrast, the white French were relatable in an absolute and almost compulsory way. This is an indictment of just how easily I acclimate to whiteness, just how "colonized" my mind is, but it isn't just me—all people of color are brainwashed into relating to colonial powers. Their normativity, our double consciousness, and our yearning to be accepted and whole, to be, essentially, de-otherized, means we "get" the colonial perspective, we can imagine it, even if we don't like it or want to. So, despite myself, it took nothing for me to conjure up and sympathize with the inner life of the bored, white French girl who rang up our coffee, or the French grannies walking around with farmer's market baskets. Even the bitchy old duck of a woman who worked at the post office, who watched me enter with a postcard, put down a few Euros, point to where a stamp would go, and say, *"Bonjour! Je suis désolé, je n'ai pas le mot . . . par avion, si'l vous plait?"*—who stood unmoving and silent, lips puckered like a drawstring purse, staring at me as if she had no idea what I could be trying to say or do at her service window—*she* was more relatable to me than the Africans who made me feel at home, even though part of her disdain may well have been a response to my blackness. It was as if dark skin was opaque to my imagination and light skin was a well-scrubbed mirror.

We returned to Italy on an evening train, tired from sleeping on cheap mattresses and, it was a delight to realize, homesick for our Florentine lives. But as soon as I returned to Italy, it felt different. Being in France had, as I say, reminded me that I was Black, that blackness was an unavoidable wrinkle in white spaces.

Now, eyes open, I began to see that the Italians had an odd way of conceptualizing blackness. With no self-consciousness, with total confidence, Italians would often ask me, *"Qual è la tua etnia?"* Whether this merely *sounded* more elegant than *What are you?* is hard to say; it's a question I, like many mixed people, are used to hearing in the United States. With white Americans, the otherizing, entitled, unsophisticated exchange often goes like this:

"So, what are you?"

Sigh. "You mean, ethnically/racially?"

"Yeah."

"I'm mixed."

"With what?"

"Black, white, and Mexican."

"Oh, yeah, I couldn't figure it out."

"Why do you ask?"

"I was just curious. It's so cool to be mixed." And sometimes, as an addendum, "I'm mixed, too, English and German."

(There is also this variant: "Where are you from?" "California." They pause, then continue: "I mean, where are your parents from?" "California and New York." They pause, then continue: "But like, before that?" "They were born there, and their parents were born in the United States, too." Long pause, "Oh."

And the far more confounding variation: "What are you mixed with besides American?")

I suppose *"Qual è la tua etnia?"* did sound more elegant, more charming, more disarming than *What are you?* because I'd almost always answer. But after *Well, my dad is Black* the Italians would cut me off happily, exclaiming something like, *Black! Che bello! Motown!* Or they'd throw their hands up joyfully and start to dance—a nod to our rhythm? Or they'd say, *I love Black people! So much life!* The Italian sense of American blackness was celebratory. They heard *Black* and their minds didn't immediately swarm with the biting, sad-faced locusts of

America's rotten habits. Initially, I loved this new paradigm. It felt like a recognition. A respect for joy; Black joy seemed innate to the Italians I met—innately comprehensible, innately whole, innately present. Or so it appeared at dinner parties and bars, over *primi piatti* and *vino*, our glasses colliding with *tings!*, cigarettes between fingers, all of us buzzed and delighted at our internationalness, each of us an Italophile (none more than the Italians themselves), and all of us bonding over the bounty of our lives. At those tables, *What are you? Oh! I love Black people!* felt as round and jammy and full of mirth as the wine we drank. I enjoyed the temporary deliverance from my own bleak narratives. I floated in the warm, unfamiliar feeling of being from a cheerful history.

Eventually, however, it began to chafe, this particular love of blackness the Italians had. It was genuine on one level; but in the same way that I genuinely love wintery weather while choosing to live on the Pacific coast, where it never snows. There was no vocabulary or curiosity among the Italians I met for learning about whole and historic American blackness. And there were no Black people *actually in* Florence. Yes, there were the requisite handfuls of blue-black African men milling around open-air markets selling soap and perfume oils. But there were no Black people in integrated, critical mass—taking up whole tables at neighborhood restaurants, trying makeup on in department stores, marrying Italians and making babies by the dozens who, though Italian, were not Italian. They were talking about blackness as seen on television, or as heard in pop music. Blackness *in theory*. Rub this warm, open profession of love up against real Black people, with living, thinking, insistent, speaking bodies—or enough Black people to impact the Italian sense of normalcy and culture—and things got more complicated, star-crossed, I think, by Italy's own colonial roots and whiteness. (Indeed, any Black person living in Italy has stories of Italian anti-Black racism.)

For instance: my Italian boyfriend, Matteo. He lived in a stately apartment on classy Via Cavour. It was a decorous, uncomfortable space with marble floors, floor-to-ceiling windows draped in folds of shantung, wrought-iron French balconies, and furniture bathed in whites and creams. His mom lived there, too. I spoke exceptional Italian and her son and I were in a serious relationship, but she rarely spoke to me directly, even when we were sitting at the same table nibbling bland breakfast cookies, or riding in the same car with Matteo, or sardined into their creaky, elegant cage of an elevator. Instead, she'd glance at me and wince, then nudge Matteo with a small elbow like a pearl onion and murmur, *Tell her to pass the bread. Tell her to put her window up. Tell her to scoot over.* One evening, in the spare living room of cream-colored linen and stone, she lifted her hands up, alarmed, and said, *Tell her not to rest her head on the couch—her hair, her hair!* She was worried my (clean) hair would soil their white upholstery. This seemed to confirm what I knew. Some element of her semi-hushed scorn had to do with my actual Blackish body emitting actual blackness in her home.

I was not experiencing a truly free form of blackness in Italy—I was experiencing an abridged, reduced, and rudimentary one. There was value in starting from an assumption of Black joy—and it was an important lesson for me on my own conception of blackness—but there was no way to proceed into anything more textured, more real. In this way, to be socially acceptable in Italy, I had to let some of my blackness go.

I also had to let go of some of my Mexican heritage. That's not Italy's fault—it's mine. I chose to trade my Spanish skills, and the key they gave me into my own history, for Italian. I learned Spanish in school, starting in second grade, and spoke it sometimes with my dad. And by the time I got to Italy, I was pretty fluent. But I couldn't hold both languages in my brain at the same time. Within a week of arriving, I observed Italian words replacing Spanish words, covering them entirely like thick paint so that I couldn't recall the Spanish word for something once I learned the Italian. I don't remember whether I had even nominal ambivalence about this exchange, though I doubt it. I was so happily strung-out on all things Italian and felt sure I'd end up living there, possibly between Italy and New York, running a gallery and married to an Italian man, speaking my beloved, idolized second-home language every day in a pasta-eating, Vespa-riding, lemon-treed paradise. In this daydream from the early part of my Italian life, race and ethnicity were neither here nor there. I barely saw this, and when I did, I saw it as a blessing ("Black! Che bello! Motown!"), not an oblivion. Instead, Italy was like a fairy tale. The vineyards! The ruins! The food! And no dark history of blackness! But, of course, an incomplete history is not a history at all.

I haven't been to Italy in fifteen years. Instead, I've been to Mexico. In law school, I discovered that Mexico was a short, cheap flight, and that I felt mellow there. I attribute this mellowness to Mexico being a brown place—I don't feel surveilled by the white gaze and its close cousin, the fatphobic gaze, when I'm there. I also attribute it to my Mexicanness, which is a mishmash of bits but also irrefutable. My dad was Mexican and Black. He was born and grew up twenty miles from the border. He treated "potatoes on the side" as anathema, and I only ever saw him order rice or tortillas. He concentrated on listening when my daughter counted in Spanish and sang to him *Los pollitos dicen pío, pío, pío*. Half his sisters identify as Hispanic. They call themselves my tias, and to them I'm "mija" (as I often was to my dad). Among the things I inherited from my dad's mom are her Spanish-language name, Savala, and her molcajete, the mortar and pestle from which she made tortillas. Her dad—my paternal great-granddad—was from Guanajuato, near San Miguel de Allende. I don't know if he was mixed, or indigenous Mexican, or related to the enslaved Africans who worked Guanajuato's rich silver mines in the 1500s and 1600s, back when Mexico was called New Spain, but an old photograph of him shows a dark man, no Europe evident in his wide-boned, widenosed face or short, dense body, brown eyes and brown skin, big hands like catchers' mitts resting on his brown suit knees.

Mexico seems to include me as I am rather than ask me to assimilate. It asks less of me than Italy and Europe did. I'm not trading part of myself to be there, and the self I naturally am—fat-ish, brown—feels like just a variation on natural human diversity rather than an outlier. During one trip, I sat on a wooden city bench watching passersby head into a Walmart-type store and noticed that muffin tops and floppy side-boob did not seem to bother anyone. Women passed in tight tank and tube tops, spaghetti straps or no straps on their almond-colored shoulders, tight denim shorts making bellies spill like foam from a beer glass, wearing bras (or not) that didn't contain or hide or even acknowledge the rolls of fat nestling under their armpits and down the sides of their rib cages. I knew I couldn't see them through anything but the lens of my Americanness—that they, in fact, might have made something entirely different of their looks, that all assessments are contextual. Nevertheless, the nonchalance of their "imperfect" bodies in public struck me. They did not seem to be making political statements about a woman's right to be saggy. They did not seem concerned about appearing well-mannered or confident or sexually available or anything, really. They just seemed like women running errands and wearing what they had on a hot June day.

Still, even with my mellow love and heritage, I'm a foreigner in Mexico. While others look fresh and dry, I sweat the garish rivers of someone who's used to fog and I carry electrolyte tabs in my purse. I'm always sick with diarrhea for a few days no matter how religiously I use bottled water to brush my teeth, wash my face, and drink. Despite sunblock, my back and forehead turn the color of raspberries. In rural areas, I'm often too tall to walk without stooping as trees seem to grow or be pruned for shorter people. I'm alarmed when Mexican police (or are those military vehicles? Cartels?) cruise the street in what look like show-of-force parades, though no one else seems to react with anxiety. But most of all, I'm a foreigner because I don't speak Spanish anymore, and I have no way to slip into life, to pour myself into Mexico seamlessly. I just have the crappy remnants of unused Italian, and the lingering prejudices that animated old choices.

I could have embraced the Mexican aspect of my identity from a younger age, and I could have thought twice about the long-term consequences of giving up Spanish, a language to which I have a generations-deep familial connection, for Italian, a language that was immensely pleasurable and useful for a short while, and now, like a vacation, simply a source of nostalgia. I wish that I had. But when and where I grew up, "Mexico" was not something to be proud of. "Mexico" was a grossly amalgamated shorthand for those parts of the Western global south that the white (and therefore normative) United States did not want, and a "Mexican" was anyone brown and speaking Spanish. I saw this in the conservative news and punditry against which my liberal mom brayed. I also saw it when my Black-and-Mexican dad climbed onto his warped, internalized-racism soapbox and called for a respectability politics among brown, Spanish-speaking people we might see around town, teenagers pushing strollers or folding burritos behind a counter. And I saw it in progressive entertainment meant for my consumption. Like *Clueless*—which was one of my favorite movies in high school—when hapless, delightful Cher assumes Lucy, her Salvadoran housekeeper, is Mexican. The housekeeper puts down her sponge and spray bottle in a huff and stamps out of the kitchen, crying, "I not a Mexican!" Lucy's sharp dismay operates on two levels: it signals the flattened conflation to which people from Mexico, Central America, and South America are subject in the United States, and it also has a nose-up air of disdain for Mexican people. Because Cher is the hapless, delightful, rich, white me I often wished to be, my forgiveness was immediate and complete. Lucy and her complaint faded quickly from memory.

"Mexican" was shorthand for maids, and for guys milling around the Home Depot parking lot, waiting to hop onto pickup beds and clean yards for cash. Mexico was the impenetrable, distant faces, noses, and mouths wrapped in red bandanas, of vegetable and fruit pickers on the drive to Fresno. (*Like my own dad*, who worked in fields picking produce throughout his childhood; the repugnance of my former internalization is not lost on me.) Mexico was why our public school had a shitty rating: ESL. Mexico was the lusty danger of *vatos* and *cholas* swarming every minute of *Dangerous Minds*, toward whom Michelle Pfeiffer's character felt both the missionary impulse and a Flora Cameronesque terror.

Mexico was also shorthand for an aggressive, smoldering sexuality we could witness in real life: see those short, dark men unloading boxes behind the grocery store—catcalling me, grinning to each other, raising their eyebrows? I was thirteen or fourteen, desperate for pale, rich Dave Heath to like me back. But it was the "Mexicans" who'd whisper to each other, call a quiet *Hey, mami* at my body, which was large and developed in the tender, childish way of puberty. This grown-man lust would have been scary and confusing no matter the men's race but, had the guys been white, it would have ultimately registered as fine instead of gross. It would have been flattering, a titillation I might scribble about in my floral, cotton-covered diary: *Someone thinks I'm pretty!* A confirmation of my ability to comply with beauty norms. Instead, I'd been taught to fear both my body and "Mexican" men—that they found me attractive only reinforced their distasteful, indecent strangeness, and mine.

Odd, though, this notion that men from Mexico, Central, and South America were sexually dangerous, harboring a power-crazed lasciviousness that made trying to screw women, or sexually harass them, a compulsion. Because it was in Italy, not Mexico, that I heard a grunting sound, saw a rocking in my peripheral left, and turned my head to catch the man across the aisle squirming and masturbating, his lanky half-cock exposed in blue cotton pants, his eyes on me and my girlfriend. And it was in Italy, not Mexico, that we came home to find a man waiting on our marble landing, somehow inside the building's entry. I'd encountered him on the block before, drunk and boorish, incoherent and horny. This time he was passed out, presumably drunk, and we turned our bodies sideways and hurried past him, our female backs sliding silent against the stone wall. And it was in Italy, not Mexico, that a man ignored my yelling and pushing, put his hands into my pants and assaulted me. I'm not saying this reveals anything about Italy; these things happen everywhere. But it's noteworthy that, throughout my late girlhood and young womanhood, I braced for the assaults of *brown* men when only *white* men had harmed me in that way—that bracing is colonialism at work.

Of course, some people get the same negative cultural messages about Mexico, Mexicans, and Central and South American people, but they also get a counterweight, something that negates or destabilizes the negative messages. I assume this comes mostly from family. These people still absorb the cultural toxins, but they also absorb the living dignity and humanity of their parents, grandparents, cousins, etc., and they end up with a more balanced view of themselves and where they come from. They also end up with a more balanced view of the world, a view that doesn't relentlessly present Europe as the cradle of beauty and class. I didn't. And because I didn't, a decade later, I thought nothing of shedding what little Mexicanness I felt for the chance to become, as I saw it, better. For the chance to belong to something with a European sheen that seemed, until my reckoning, to accept me.

After my dad died—and fifteen years after I left Italy for good—I started to seriously consider how I once spoke Spanish and my own Mexicanness, what it meant to be Mexican, how constricted my view of brown Mexico was under the mental and emotional rule of white normativity, and whether, as a way of remembering him and becoming myself, I could make Mexico part of my life. Lineage matters to me. *My* lineage, and also future lineage, what my daughter will have. Our lineage keeps us tethered safely to the world. But my curiosity and longing are too late, and too little. I'm nearly (perhaps already) middle-aged. I am very white, in many ways. I'm very Black in many ways, too. I'm entrenched in my current self. There isn't much room in me left for other things. It feels like any Mexicanness I cultivate now will be, indeed, *cultivated*, and thin. The sources of cultural identity are no longer open to me the way they once were.

I had an encounter, though, that left me wondering whether one even needs external sources of cultural identity when the actual ties that bind you are internal—in your family, in your genes. An older repairman came to finish a job on our heater. His gray jumpsuit said *Luis*. He had a dense accent, and a handsome smile that made his crow's feet move around his eyes in a dancerly way. We waited at the dining room table for the county inspector to arrive. Luis accepted a cup of coffee. He studied me and said, to my shock and delight, "Are you Latina?" This had never happened before. I grinned. I laughed. "Yes!" I paused. "Well, Afro-Latina. That's my dad. He was Black and Mexican." I pointed to a photograph. I'm not sure what *Afro-Latina* might have meant to him, but given that I don't speak Spanish I wanted to insert a speedbump, slow any assumption he might have about my cultural fluency and authenticity. He stood up and pointed at the photo, his nail rimmed dark with work grease. "This is your father?" "Yes. And that's his mom and his grandparents. Black and Mexican." Luis said, "Ah, I see. I thought with your name, your face, maybe you might be." Which, since I don't speak Spanish, is how I now fundamentally think of my own Mexicanness—maybe you might be.

To reclaim my most potent connection to my Mexican heritage, which dwells intertwined with my Black heritage, I'd also have to relearn Spanish and, reluctantly, unlearn Italian. Because I still can't hold both languages. When I make forays into learning Spanish, the Italian I remember quickly disintegrates. It's one or the other, and I've yet to make the choice that seems, in light of where I'm from and where I live, obvious: *speak Spanish*. Having a young child, for whom the sources of cultural identity are wide open, ought to make this decision—Italy vs. Mexico—simple. It doesn't. I'm stuck. Partly because I still love Italian, partly because I prize my former fluency, and partly because, unless I move to a Spanish-speaking country, I doubt I'll ever be as fluent in Spanish as I was in Italian; why give up excellence, even former excellence, for mediocrity?

But isn't that just it—this question of excellence and mediocrity sprawls far beyond linguistic skills and into the vast, murky terrain of bias. Because I cannot guarantee that my white-centric upbringing isn't also a factor. I can't guarantee that the colonialism that shaped my taste is gone. The European mystique—of sophistication, refinement, of history itself—endures, and gives Italy and its language bonus points. Points it may not deserve. Mexican Spanish doesn't strike my ear as melodic and elegant the way Italian does; it does not feel like a perfect architecture of grammar and sound—is this a neutral assessment, or just the unsurprising result of racialized hierarchy, under which nothing brown can be as good as anything white? Mexico doesn't have the reputation for art, natural beauty, culture, cuisine, and style that Italy does; again—objective assessment, or no? Because love affairs, like what I had (and Americans have) with Italy, are never objective. Neither are assessments of value, contribution, and merit. Italy is fabulous; Europe is fabulous; but they and their offerings to humanity are not inarguably superior to the people and places of lower longitudes. Maybe they're just whiter, and therefore imbued with an unfair legibility. Maybe they're just what I was taught to want.

The Body Endures

What happens to burdens? I have some. I wonder: do they weld themselves to each other, grow thicker and denser, cleaving to our bodies with keloid seams? Because this coalescence, this mounting and merging would explain why my hips hurt the week of my daughter's birthday, the week I spent in the hospital, wrecked and apart from her. Why my back hurts the month my dad died. Why the news sometimes makes my thigh bones shake and scrape against my knees. Why I take a hot, salty bath every night; to wash off the stickiness that has amassed, some of it old, antebellum and farther back, cobwebbed and preverbal, grandmothers' and great-grandmothers'. Yes, I think burdens collect. They are the body itself; please don't call me strong. I think, eventually, when there are enough of them, they join hands, get drunk and rowdy and clamor for contact with your skin, your bones. They're coming for you, and maybe, if you can decipher it, there's some wisdom on their lips; but also some blood—yours. This is why I ache just walking. This is why I daydream. This is why I flake. This is why I have secrets. This is why I'm silent. This is why I just want to sleep. This is inescapable. This is work.

* * *

I'm sure there is another, normal, low-class Big Sur set way back from the ocean, tucked into dark canyons, where modest houses battle mildew and laundromat coins collect in jars. But here at this sumptuous seaside estate, which I am privileged enough to have access to, I only experience the rich, clean spaciousness of Big Sur, and it allays how drained and spent I feel. Big Sur! With its midnights an absolute, velvet dark; its chalky cliffs tumbling down to meet the teal thrash of Pacific waves; its forest groves like cathedrals, holding quiet; how the air smells of fog and woodsmoke, pine and salt! My body feels, for the first time in years, restful. Full of rest. My anxiety fades. I revere the magnitude of the world in peace.

Still, I'm here for a wedding, so I know it's coming—

It's coming—

It's—

Picture time! "We're doing photos, everyone!" We line up. We're grinning. We all jut our arms out, broken-doll style, and laugh. The bride most saucily of all, and I think she says *Well, duh, I want my arm to look thin, obvi!* She says it with a smile, good-natured. Other women agree; the groom's mom, his sister, some of the bride's friends. I suppose even I agree. I make like my shoulder is broken and my arm shoots out at that hard, enchanting angle. Whatever thinness my current arm can approximate is here in this broken-doll pose. The sun is hot under these oak trees; my heels sink into the wet ground; at last a breeze comes off the ocean and it's a blue reprieve on the back of my neck. I try to point my chin slightly down as a photographer taught me. It's slimming. I imagine seeing the pictures in a few weeks and being elated and relieved that I don't look fat. This won't happen, though, because my arm can't be slimmed with a camera trick. Mine is a thick arm, thick like a prosciutto. It's a carrier of toddlers and wiggly, shining stretch marks, a schlepper of grocery bags and umbrellas and briefcases and laundry baskets; a treasure chest of sunlight and freckles.

I won't ask these women to be less fatphobic. Instead, I do the broken doll. I also slump, sliding down the wall of myself until, on the inside, I'm poured into my pinching shoes and I'm nose-down on the ground, very tired again. I feel a bit violated by their fatphobia, but also to blame. It's like the summer of 1999, the first summer I ever wore a tank top in public: the sun's alchemy on that long-hidden skin, the warm wind touching it in the dissolving evening light. And a man sat too close to me in the empty movie theater and began to masturbate, and I wondered if it was because of my arms, whether my body was too available even if it wasn't desirable, whether my arms' fleshiness gave him permission.

I have had this memory of a belly following me around. It presses against me, just out of sight, murmuring for attention, and for months I can't place it, or reach it, and it lingers like an itch, and then I remember: "Sometimes." The Britney Spears song, that video. It debuted on *Total Request Live*. I noticed Britney's fake tan, her beguilingly arched feet when she's sitting baseball-capped on the beach, how she brings the tip of her tongue to the roof of her mouth on *l* sounds, making them pinkly pornographic, how she twitches her glossed lips to mirror her vocal runs, how she can make her eyes faintly, just barely begin to cross, and it makes her face cute and doltish.

But really it was her belly that got me. Such tenderness. Such innocence. Her belly was like the warm top of a vanilla cake when it comes out of the oven. It was bright and optimistic and sexy. Softly flat. After seeing that video, I started spending four hundred dollars every week on my trainer at Crunch; this, I know, was a privilege. The privilege of excess money, of excess time. When I began specifying my goals and how I wanted particular body parts to look, he interrupted by putting his hand up and saying, "I know just the body you want. I got this." The first week my arms trembled when I put my coat on. My core felt stabbed when I coughed. He coached me to stop eating salt; to keep nothing but cold cuts in the fridge; to, once a week, "spike" my metabolism with a huge, sugary, carby meal. He suggested I switch from 100 ounces of water each day to 100 ounces of green tea. Once, he caught me eating pizza on a Friday night and then French toast the next day. He shook his head and threw up his hands, looking pissed. *Some people just don't want to be helped!* I did want help, but it was never enough. It never totally worked. My body never became or felt as bright and optimistic and innocent and sexy as what I saw in "Sometimes." My body always felt old and un-right. Boobs too soon, stretch marks too soon and in the wrong places (insides of my arms, tops of my shoulders). Butt kind of mom-ish and flat "like two buttermilk biscuits"— that is what the guys behind me on the stairs said, laughing to themselves. So, I watched that video a thousand times, rubbing Britney's belly on my cheeks like a bar of soap. I wanted her belly because I wanted a chance—even just a *chance*—at a body that is nearly aromatic with daffy, cute, cross-eyed perfection. Her body and its unalloyed (normative) beauty seemed potent and effortless, and not, as mine sometimes did, worn-out with the aspiration and effort of outrunning my genes.

A few families we know are sharing a vacation house on a lake and someone has the idea to rent a party boat. (Lucky me, indeed; I sat on the deck and drank wine and gazed at the stars and thanked God for my life.) We meet at the dock after our eggs-and-pastries breakfast, the sun clear over the pines and the snowmelt-lake frigid enough to hurt our bones. All night before and all morning I worry about the single step I'll have to take from the floating dock onto the boat. I'm the heaviest person on our trip. The stern will probably dunk when I get on. Everyone will observe this. Which is better, meaning more subtle: to have people feel it but not see it because I'm the last to board? Or to have people see it but not feel it because I'm first? The kids won't notice, laughing about how their life jackets have a third strap that goes between their legs, giddy about the turtles and fish near the shore. But the adults will notice, and even though these are my friends and family, they love and like me, and they believe they are immune from this stuff, they are also part of this culture, so they will think *fat*, and I will feel reduced and afraid of repercussions.

Like when John, my husband, kept wanting to kayak on our lavish honeymoon in Jamaica. Finally I agreed. We crossed the hot sand and approached the boat guys sitting on driftwood logs and staring at their phones. I decided to make it a joke. I laughed and said, "Um, ha ha, is there a weight limit for these things?" The boat guy and my husband stared blankly at me. "Like, what if it sinks. If we're too heavy?" The boat guy, bending to push the kayak from the sand into the water, shook his head. I whispered to my husband, "Do you think I'm too heavy for it?" Firmly, he said, "No." I stepped into the kayak, felt it bob and tilt, and we cast off. The kayak did not sink. We went far into the bay, saw starfish and private beaches and let our legs dangle in the aquamarine warmth of the Caribbean Sea. But the memory is still tainted with all that peppery fear, so stubborn, arms crossed and unmoved by my hope.

Tuesday, November 8, 2016. Election Day. Dinnertime. I bring buttered peas and fish sticks and tomatoes to the table. I light a candle and think about the passage of time as I hear the silverware drawer slide crankily open and my daughter, who was only toddling when we moved here, rummage for a fork. I'm grateful for my life. The dark at the windows makes our home feel cozy and content. Our neighborhood is safe and nice looking, with western views of the ocean and eastern views of a massive, rolling state park. The schools are decent, the neighbors friendly. We come to the table each night with fresh and plentiful food. My husband sits at the head. I both like this—a small proof of how well I've put together a mainstream life, the peculiar, tight-corset comfort of old-school gender norms—and dislike it: Why shouldn't *I* sit at the head of the damn table? I run this house!

"So, when did you end up voting today?" I ask.

Later, I would sit on the couch, double-screening PBS on television and the *New York Times* website, and watch dumbstruck as the *Times'* election predictor flipped on its head, hugging a pillow to my chest, feeling the rise of dread (though not exactly surprise or shock) until my beloved, pearl-and-twinset Judy Woodruff called it.

"I didn't, actually."

"You didn't what?" I pause with a hand hovering over the tomatoes, feeling my pulse pick up, as if it's had a premonition.

"I didn't vote."

"You didn't vote?"

"I didn't want to deal with the wait after work, I wanted to get home."

"So, you didn't vote in this election?"

He shrugs. "And I knew it wouldn't matter." Living in California, as we do.

I put a couple tomato slices on my plate, jewel-toned yellow and ruby, a miracle of late heirlooms, slick with olive oil and sprinkled with salt. "You didn't vote." I say it again. Philosophically, to myself, as if it is a puzzling sidenote. But I am already astounded, panicking, smashed up; it's just that my voice is calm. Our kid is with us, smooshing panko'ed halibut into her teeth and laughing. "Mama, look."

"I see, honey."

Later that night, I'm awake in bed, staring at the sleet-colored bay water beyond the cypress trees, a clot of nausea below my ribs. I did not say good night to my husband or accept his kiss, really, just jutted my cheek and jaw toward him so he could peck it. I hope (stupidly) that my silence and withdrawal will enlighten him and I'll wake to an earnest apology. The bay is flat. There are no boats or white sails on the water. The yellow specks of city lights feel far away and fleeting. The view is silent at two a.m. A tip of red bridge spire pops up from the fog. I roll onto my side, grab the metal mixing bowl I'd brought to bed with me, and vomit.

My husband cannot viscerally understand the challenges of Black womanhood, mixed Black womanhood, fat womanhood, and motherhood—the anxieties that lurch and careen in our skulls, the sliding cliffs on which we walk, the traps set on our own front porches, the clenching with fear, the grinding and near-constant production of acceptability. My husband can't jump bodies and gene pools and tall epigenetic mountains to understand this like I do. I don't expect him to. But as I walk my bowl of vomit to the toilet and flush it down, wipe my face, hear the ruffle of his snores from our bedroom, I wonder with vinegary anger what it might take—more than marrying me, a woman of color? More than having a brown daughter? More than having a Black father-in-law and brother-in-law and sister-in-law?—for him to wake up, to be engaged. To feel the ropey burns of his own skin in the game now, too. To understand that his wife and daughter's bodies—and therefore his heart—have only a precarious freedom.

We're heading north on Highway 80 and almost at the Carquinez Bridge, the C&H sugar factory's brick warehouse to the east and brown, late-summer hills to the west. Acoustic Eric

Clapton is on the radio. *Laaaaayla.* My husband drives. We're on our way to a family gathering at my uncle's, grilled salmon and a firepit at sunset over the marsh. I'm stuck on something I heard; I turn back toward my mom, who rides in the back next to the car seat. "Did you hear about that recording? Nixon and Governor Reagan?" She shakes her head. "Reagan calls Black people monkeys and says something like, *They're not even comfortable wearing shoes yet.* And they laugh, like *Just emerged from the jungle, ha ha ha!*" I make a sound like a tycoon, a couple jolly old fellows, chins tucked in, brandy in their snifters, guffawing. My mom shakes her head slowly. I say, "I know. Same old shit." A mile or so later I'm still thinking about it, and the recent mass shootings in El Paso and other parts of West Texas, and I say, "That recording? *That's* the kind of thing that makes you want to get your AK-47." My mom jumps in, "I was just thinking that! Line 'em up out back and shoot 'em." Half singsong and nodding toward our toddler in her car seat, my husband scolds, "Language, we don't shoot people . . ." I tense up. "I can say AK-47. She doesn't know what that means." He switches lanes without the blinker. My mom says, "No, John, you're right, I hear you. I shouldn't have said that." I'm still annoyed, though, and I say, "My mom went too far. But I'm perfectly allowed to say what I said. *Obviously* I don't mean it literally. But I'm not taking it back." He doesn't answer. I want to say something about the balance: when you're raising a girl, and when you're raising a child of color, there is a *balance* between preparing them for the world's assaults and keeping their innocence intact. I want to say that I'm on it and I don't need chastising. I'm thinking of these things in a particular way that he, as a white guy, is not. And he should let me decide what my brown daughter needs to hear about the world. I don't say anything. But I think, *He didn't even vote*.

I'm the executive director. I speak first, introducing our esteemed guest and then returning to my seat. The arms of the seat are tight on my flesh. The crowd is small but we warned her it would be. She points her red laser dot at the screen and tells us about women of color in legal academia. She's interviewed many law professors who are also women and nonwhite. Their experience is the topic of her new book. Among other slights and unfair topographies, they describe, again and again, being students' "law mom." Students arrive in their offices, sighing and letting their backpacks slide to the floor, as if they are too exhausted to *set them* there, and want hugs, comfort, candies from the dish, reassurance, mentorship. To be sure, she says, this is in part a positive sign that students, especially female students and students of color, consciously bond with their female professors of color. But it is also a sign of how people, including students, unconsciously read women of color as available for mothering and caretaking. The "law mom" role is rewarding, yes, but it also puts an uncompensated demand on members of the faculty who are already working under the weight of unique biases. There are sounds of recognition in the audience. Snaps and a couple claps. I look around, confused and slightly alarmed; I have taken pride in being a "law mom" to students. I've felt energized and useful when they come to me, cry or vent or ask for a hug. It's been part of what makes my job good. But this new way of seeing their affection—seeing it as a tainted result of Mammy's eternal presence in our lizard brains instead of undiluted respect and connection—makes me cringe at my own stupidity. I feel an arrow of mortification pierce some bubble over my head. A thought bubble that said *My students love me.* How obtuse can I be? I lapped up this approval, this being needed, when I maybe should have seen it as part of my own subjugation. And my fellow women of color seem already to have figured this out; maybe my whiteness is blinding me, or if not my own whiteness, my acclimation to whiteness in general. Maybe my ability to meld into whiteness has done me wrong here, leaving me both undefended and unfrightened. I feel, and fear, a schism within myself.

I'm in front of the refrigerated case at the cute, overpriced market where I sometimes pick up last-minute groceries, my beat-up car sliding in among Benzes and Audis. A lady approaches me and my green basket. I'd put her post-menopausal but not old. Short brown hair, leather mocs, khaki pants, and an ironed button-down. She's white. She asks me if I can reach something. I say, "Hmm?" She repeats, "Could you reach up there and get that for me?" I look where she is pointing. Some glass jars of expensive yogurt. Opening the cold-case door, reaching up, feeling the bigness of my body, the brown of it, how maybe it reminds her of some childhood caretaker, I say, "You know, I don't work here." My voice is testy as I hand her the jar. She says, "Of course I know that, I know that." I believe her. She says, "Thank you, very very much, thank you so very much for that."

I shouldn't have been so hard on her. People ask each other for favors. I'm tall and I can reach the top shelf. I carry my annoyance and regret into the checkout line, making sure to be upbeat and polite with the cashier in case the lady is watching, had been going on to herself about my attitude. *I can't understand why they are just so difficult!* Like when a white lady asked me to walk her package into the post office so she didn't have to park her car. She could see I was heading there myself. And I started to say yes. But then I rolled my eyes and said no, walking away mad. She looked so hurt, so confused, and I felt her struggle to understand. I could have helped; but what did she see when she looked at me that made her ask?

And what about privilege? That well-coiffed, white-gloved cousin of burdens, riding in a carriage and wrapped in lavender satin, an amused smirk on its face. I have some of that, too. All this privilege makes life easier in many ways, but not in every way. My privilege is unreliable. It flakes on me. I can ask it to do something—stand between me and that lady at the grocery store who pointed to the high shelf, maybe—but it will generally shrug and tell me no. I think privilege like mine—the kind that coalesces around an otherwise marginalized body—is fundamentally weak. It doesn't want to put itself on the line. And that is the very soul of privilege—not having to work if you don't feel like it—so it shouldn't surprise me. Still, it's always a revelation when the privilege I have doesn't fully protect me from the burdens, doesn't protect me the way, say, my husband's white male privilege seems to. That, for example, even with my money and education and light skin, I am *still* three times more likely to die in childbirth than a white woman, and so is my child, because we're Black. That, for example, even with the cushy life I lead (my job, my house—all opulent by any global scale), I know I'm not deeply safe in "Trump's America," and I can't for a second imagine not voting. That even with the money to pay a trainer's exorbitant fees, my body will never comply enough, will always be subject to the harms of fatphobia, some of which can be empirically measured and some of which cannot. This is why I think it comes down to the body. Whatever else life hands you, your body fundamentally protects and shields you, or is fundamentally a target. So I turn to my privilege for help, I entreat it for assistance, but often it just continues playing, capricious and self-absorbed; that's its prerogative, that's its very essence. No matter how privileged I get, with my fat-ish, Black, female body, the burdens are always nipping at my heels. The body is inevitable. It can't be masked. For better and worse, the body endures.

Fat in Ways White Girls Don't Understand

I'm fat in ways that white girls don't understand. I'm fat in ways that my white mom didn't understand, and still doesn't; nearing eighty, she diets and rebels, diets and rebels, still trapped in the cycle of perfecting, or at least improving, her body, still riding the cycle's restrictions and hopes and the impending fall off the wagon. When she sleeps at our house, she sometimes waits until the lights are out, then pads to the kitchen and eats more, leaning alone against the counter. At Thanksgiving, the table in candlelight, she says, "Starting tomorrow, no more sugar and no more junk." These are things I have done, too. She is my mom; I wish she were free.

I'm fat in ways only Black girls understand. For us, it's less about the number and more about how you carry it. We originated *thick*, tied to patriarchy though the concept is. We are often allowed an embodied-ness that they don't let our white sisters play with much. White girls are supposed to quick-toss fat as if it were hot potatoes, like they're scared of being burned. But we can often just get on with our lives, fat and all.

For example: Barb, my white aunt, the one who married into the family, sees me at Christmas and winces. She says, "You just keep getting bigger!" It's true, I do; I get fatter and fatter, don't I? I am ten years old. But my Black auntie, auntie-by-blood Renee, stands on her stucco stoop in a warm, smoggy Los Angeles neighborhood and, seeing us emerge from the de ville after the drive from San Francisco, cries to twelve-year-old me, "Oh, you beautiful Amazon!" (Sweet Renee, my dad's favorite, who wore a pink satiny house dress and cooked us scrambled eggs at midnight. I remember the orange coil of the electric stove under the nonstick pan into which she dropped a glug of canola oil. I remember her dry heels in lavender slippers that slapped the linoleum, and her dimpled, silky arms as she stroked my wooly hair—which the white kids called a Brillo pad.)

And yet, though blackness can make it easier to be fat, part of my fat-body shame is because I'm Black: fat Black women make us—make you—think of Mammy. Mammy has a job. Her job is to play a crushingly subservient, domestic role in our stories, imaginations, myths, histories, and futures. Her job is to remind us of how white women and Black women differ. To borrow from scholar Sabrina Strings, her job is to denigrate (fat) Black women (*see what you are?*) and to keep white women in line (*you don't want to be that, do you?*).* Her role is to be ir-reconcilable with the ideal of womanhood, which is to say, the ideal of *white* womanhood, a lady who is immaculate, charming,

---

* From *Fearing the Black Body: The Racial Origins of Fat Phobia* by Sabrina Strings.

thin, fragile, and, of course, ornamentally beautiful. Mammy is so unwomanly that to be her, or like her, is to be an unwoman. Like a linebacker in lipstick, or a pig. Fat Black women are mashed into the grotesque shape of Mammy and then baked in the kiln of racism; at least, that's what they try to do to us.

There's nothing inherently servile or low in the individual or combined characteristics of fatness, blackness, and womanhood. But the confluence of these characteristics makes Mammy a potent cautionary tale and a person for whom upward mobility is not even a dream, let alone a possibility: she's fat, and therefore (supposedly) undesirable; she's Black, and therefore (supposedly) simple and animalistic; and she's a woman, and therefore (supposedly) obedient and submissive. She acts as a neutered, voiceless servant who can only function in the domestic sphere at the service of real women, and real men. Imagine the impossibility of Mammy the Neuroscientist! Or Mammy the Mayor! Or Mammy the pageant queen, or gifted writer, or beloved wife—you can't. The triad of her defining qualities—fat, Black, female—won't let her do anything with her life but domestic labor. Watch as she manages all kinds of house-bound tasks: making pancakes and scrubbing tile, washing a child's fine hair and mending torn doll clothes.

Domestic labor is the work we honor least. It's the work we don't value and often don't pay, sometimes refuse even to see. It's caring for children, for the elderly, for the sick and the well. It's vile: picking hardened food off pans with fingernails, scrubbing smears of shit from the toilet bowl, sniffing clothes to see if they're dirty, emptying trash bins of wax-caked Q-tips and bloody tampons. It's also pleasurable: roasting crispy-skinned chicken and gold potatoes, icing three-layer cakes for birthdays, pouring warm bathwater down a toddler's back, smoothing fresh sheets across mattresses, picking garden flowers for a vase. Vile or pleasurable, this work is devalued. I can't help that my large, Black, vagina-having body is inscribed with this vile and pleasurable work. I can't help that my body may read like a Mammy to you. But I'm as vain as any woman must be (NARS Jungle Red, Louis Vuitton bag, shaved pits and all that). I'm as acculturated to free-market capitalist patriarchy as anyone. So why would I want to trigger thoughts of shuffling, domestic labor when I walk into a room? *I don't*, but trigger them I do. Or I fear I do, and what is the difference? I am fat, Black, and female. The gap between what I fear and what is real is thin and permeable, the site of constant osmosis.

When I stride to the podium (heels clicking) to begin my remarks or convene a meeting at the head of the table (the boss doesn't take notes so I don't have a pen), I feel not only my genuine me-ness, of which I am proud, but my Mammy-ness. I feel *you* feeling my Mammy-ness, too. I feel her and it and you every day; not all day every day, but every day.

She is the part of fat Black womanhood that I don't like. (Or should I say *you* are the part I don't like, you who created and re-create Mammy with your lack of imagination, your lack of critical analysis?) She's not to blame; she isn't even real. But I do blame her. That's how it works. She's how I'm fat in ways that white girls don't understand.

If I were a better person, instead of scheming ways to destroy her, I'd ask Mammy what her name is and offer her something to drink. If I were brave, I'd take her picture, one of her alone, portrait-like. I'd like to sit with her on a porch swing that is strong enough to hold our body weights, and be silent, watching the tides in the distance speckle and flow under sunlight. If I were more kind, I'd honor her in the tiny bourgeois ways of which I'd be capable, like wearing a bikini to the public pool. I'd see her eyes; what color and shape are they? Small and green like mine? Or maybe brown, like my sister's? And I would bear witness to the light on her face and the expressions on her face that are human, only human, as fully human as mine, and yours. And I'd tell the world.

Little Satin Bomber Body

I still remember my cropped bomber jacket, thin black satin with a silver zipper, more of a blouse than a coat. I found it at that vintage shop on Broadway, the one near where Claire Danes grocery shopped, by that club on a side street where everyone did lines off the bar at last call. I remember shrugging a much smaller me into this jacket, little shoulders, little waist. When I zipped it, the hem hugged me just below my ribs—and it felt good to know my limit, where my body ended, and that it ended at all. I remember how my boobs looked in the satin bomber, jaunty and small, no bra or shirt, and the zipper undone halfway.

I remember the whole outfit the first time I wore the jacket: juniors-section Levi's with tiger stripes of indigo across my hips. Silver D'Orsay pumps, Manolo-looking but cheap, with a costume brooch at the toes. My thick hair parted in the middle, straight, and long to my elbows. The fat guy at Mo' Betta salon said, "*Mmmm!* That's a lot of natural hair, girl," as he slid the stinking flat iron down my tawny strands.

We took a photo that night, me and my girlfriends, with a roll-of-film camera, arms around each other in our East Village dorm, getting ready to give Manhattan a sexy, joyful kind of hell while our roommates and their friends settled in on the couch for a long night of weed. (One of the friends was a blond actor with a beauty mark above his lip. He was in commercials that were the early-aughts equivalent of a meme and sort of famous. He came over sometimes to buy weed, and I was determined to hook up with him. It would signal, I thought, a victory—proof of my smallness. Eventually, I sort of did. We planted a series of muddled kisses on each other's lips during Eighties Night at Don Hill. His eyes were heavy-lidded as he rubbed an intoxicated, indifferent hand on my chest and back. I felt nothing at all, totally gripped by whether he could feel the ribs beneath my skin, hopeful that he could.)

That night, in my little satin bomber and cheap heels, I stood outside a bar on East-something, feeling giddy, fully grown, and inevitable with my friends; it was the kind of night when New York is the city you came looking for, and you're on the verge of everything exciting (love, fame). No cars drive down the block and it feels like a movie set, and you're happily conscious of how you look in the streetlight, you and the boys and girls around you, drunk and exhaling Marlboro Red Os, flush with immortality.

This guy Connor I'd known for a while nodded at my half-down zipper and, with cool, understated appreciation, said, "That's nice." I grinned and looked down. "What, this?" I said. He nodded, crushing ice cubes in his teeth. "Just sexy enough," he said. We never hooked up, he and I.

When I developed the photos from that night, I was excited to see my collarbones lifting up and away! And my arms, even in the jacket, were as lanky as a boy's. Those body parts were my test: collarbones and arms. My goal: late-nineties Gwen Stefani, with her chest tucked in, upper back a little rounded, and her clavicle and shoulders jutting out with insouciant innocence—"What? Who, me?" Some nights, I used chestnut eyeshadow to draw those bones out more.

Another night in Manhattan, I met Mira at the Vietnamese restaurant where she hosted and got us all free drinks. I wore a white wisp of a bra from the Gap and a wife-beater. Deep in my subclinical eating disorder, I was thrilled when I outed my collarbones and let my arms dangle a bit. Catching my reflection behind the bar, I said, "Oh my god, look at my arms." Mira said, "I know, you look great." I said, "I'm really doing this." Mira swigged her cocktail. "I know," she said. "You look great."

I still think about the black satin bomber body and that New York City year, my thinnest ever. It didn't last. (Who can subsist on aerosol whipped cream and sliced turkey?) But I always believed I'd get back to those skinny times, and so I carried the bomber with me from New York to DC to Italy to California, undergrad to first job, last job to grad school. I put it on periodically to check how I was doing—fat, thin, fat, thin, two-sided like the chaos-control Kandinsky. ("What makes it exceptional is that Kandinsky painted on either side of the canvas in two radically different styles. One wild and vivid, the other somber and geometric." / "We flip it around for variety. Chaos, control. Chaos, control. You like? You like?" From *Six Degrees of Separation*.)

Kendall, my best friend, finally said, "Aw, give it to Goodwill for some skinny kid to wear." We were old enough to think of the people we'd been as kids.

It was hard to throw the jacket away. The garment—which I used as a measuring stick, as a goal, as punishment—didn't exactly *spark joy*, but it was pure potential, each thread glowing with the promise of past and future thinness. Eventually, while stuffing a trash bag with spring cleaning, I tossed in the silky bomber. It sat on top, I knotted the bag, and then, eight years after it no longer fit, it was gone.

I still sometimes dream of a different body. In the future, I imagine family and friends applauding me when I'm thin again. *Good job!* they'll say. *Wow! Well done!* I imagine walking to the stage for graduation, where I give remarks, up the steps and to the podium, and the audience noticing how slim I am; how my fatness and blackness no longer potentiate each other, and I'm no longer doubly exiled among my thin, white colleagues. I imagine them nodding with approval that I'm no longer fat, when I've finally gotten rid of that thing, like a long mullet, or a ratty fur jacket, or sneakers with separating soles. For now, I put pictures up from thinner days so when people visit they know that I used to be thin.

Not long ago, my godfather sat me down. He said, "It took you a year to gain weight and have your daughter. It's been over a year since she was born, and it seems you ought to be losing it now." We were having breakfast at the little cafe he likes, near the golf club, strong coffee and good avocado with the omelets. I smiled brightly, imagining pinning my cheeks up, Lillian Gish-like. I said, "Yes, that's true, and I'm going to get back into taking care of myself." "Good!" he said, that settled.

Telling him that I've stopped dieting—I'm determined never to go back to it—was impossible. *I don't diet anymore, Papa Mac, so I may never lose weight.* He wouldn't understand any more than I understand, really, a female Trump voter. Which is to say, this vivid, prismatic Pangea I've discovered outside the cave, this crew of renegade women in the wilderness, building big fires and stone cairns and hollering at the moon, jumping the outlines of mountains and laughing in the rivers, who've felt liberation, who've sucked it into themselves and blown it back out to others like the blast of fog horns, who've dug pitch-black graves and dropped the jangling ropes of dieting into them, and pissed on them, who are fat and happy, fat and free, doing just fine . . . This place is illegible to him; and sometimes to me, though I live there now, fat as a motherfucker, or at least I live close enough to smell the smoke from their campfires and see the firelight through the pines, and to hear them calling *Over here! Come on!* every day and night.

Author's Note

This book is memoir and therefore based on what I recall. That said, memory and impressions can be fallible, and interpretations can differ. I've tried to let readers know when I'm especially aware that others may or do recall events differently. Additionally, in this book, I write about my great-great-grandmother, Laura, who was killed by white supremacists in Texas. It's not the first time I've written about her—in 2020, *Vogue* published an essay about her death on their online opinion page. Between publication of that piece and this book, and with the help of the genealogists at Lineages, new information about Laura's last day came to light. When I wrote the *Vogue* piece, my family's belief was that Texas Rangers killed Laura while her husband was at work; genealogists, however, found newspaper articles reporting that Laura's husband was home, and that she was killed not by Texas Rangers but by a faction of the White Cappers, a white supremacist, vigilante gang in the mold of the Ku Klux Klan. Like the Klan, the White Cappers took it upon themselves to enforce laws, harass and intimidate Black people, and maintain both de jure and de facto racial hierarchy. Aside from these differences, the stories are the same: a woman was terrified, a racist murder occurred, and a family was changed forever. In some ways, the details are worse—I learned, for instance, that the crime scene was, according to the reporter, beyond description. As one of Laura's descendants—one who is, like her, a Black woman and a mother—the more I learn about her death the harder it is to metabolize. The omnipresence of white supremacy and her vulnerability as a woman are inexorable, and they echo into my own life, and my daughter's. On a purely personal level, I sometimes wish I could unlearn Laura's story. As a writer and thinker, though, this particular experience of finding and telling family history has been valuable. For one thing, it's shown me that our histories, especially involving race, are complex and always unfolding: mine includes not just what happened to Laura, but how the story was told across generations, what was recorded by external sources, what was lived by each person in the room, and what I now do with it. Grappling with Laura's story means bringing these threads together and letting them point toward a whole; in this case, some of the details shift depending on whose recollection is centered but the core emotional truth and its position within our larger American history are inescapable. Grappling with Laura's story has also meant being willing to learn things I didn't want to, and things that were different than what I thought. This, I think, is probably true of all family histories involving race. The tangled intricacies of these stories—including how we learn them, or why we're sheltered from them—isn't a reason to turn away. It's a reason to go deeper.

Acknowledgments

One of the unexpected joys of making a book has been witnessing how collaborative the process is. Many people helped me through each layer of creation and I'm thrilled to thank them here.

Thank you, forever, to my one-of-a-kind parents, Susie Scholefield and Lee Roy Nolan. I give extra, exuberant thanks to my mom, who has been reading my writing and encouraging it mightily since I was a little girl.

I'm eternally thankful to Farley Chase, my dear agent, for shepherding this childhood dream, for his enthusiastic, insightful attention the first time my writing appeared in his inbox (and every time thereafter), and for his savvy, big-hearted counsel. He's been my champion and my rock through the thick and thin of writing this book.

I'm also eternally thankful to Dawn Davis, my superlative editor, for her cheerleading, her incisive questions, and her artfully raised eyebrow when she knew a passage could be better. She powerfully sharpened these essays while still honoring my (occasionally wild) vision and instincts.

This book would not exist without Jill Leovy, whose friendship and mentorship I am lucky to have. I'll be thanking her forever.

Thank you to Emily Simonson, my ninth-inning editor, for her deft guidance and warmth. And thanks to Cat Boyd, Alicia Brancato, Jessica Chin, Chelcee Johns, Carly Loman, Leila Siddiqui, and the entire Simon & Schuster team for the work that happens alongside the writing, from copyediting to publicity. Special thanks to Zoe Norvell for cover art that took my breath away.

Thank you to the many people who read early drafts, urged me onward, or otherwise displayed deep generosity of knowledge and spirit in key moments. I'd especially like to thank, in nearly alphabetical order, Kenda Greenwood Moran (*primus inter pares*), Alexandra Accornero, Sherry Azimi, Rashida Bumbray, Diana DiGennaro, Betty Jo Gallardo, Fanna Gamal, Biambu Garrett (my big brother), Sarah Lotus Garrett (my big sister), Jessica Guzman, Christy Harrison, Rujeko Hockley, Alexa Kielty, Alexa Koenig, Laura Lee Mattingly, Christian Miller, Lindsay Nako, Jenna Otten, Seema Patel, Ashley Renteria, Quinn Rotchford, Melody Morgan Sorensen, Anjali Srinivasan, and my godfather, Willie Mac Thompson. Also in this category are the many people who gave me their blessing as I wrote my take on our shared experiences.

Thank you to Mesa Refuge and Tiffany Golden for two peaceful, productive weeks in Point Reyes, CA, during which this manuscript coalesced into a whole.

Thank you to my supportive Berkeley Law colleagues, with particular gratitude going to Ian Haney López. Many thanks,

ACKNOWLEDGMENTS

as well, to UC Berkeley's library staff, and to the librarians, archivists, and map specialists at the Library of Virginia.

Special thanks to Lisa Arrastia, my high school English teacher. Her ardent belief in the power of words, including mine, let me imagine myself as a writer.

Finally, thank you to John, my husband, whose steadiness, calm, and wonderful fathering created the quiet space in our home for me to write this book, and to our daughter, Gemma, my pride and my joy.

About the Author

Savala Nolan is a writer, speaker, and lawyer. She is executive director of the Thelton E. Henderson Center for Social Justice at University of California, Berkeley, School of Law. She and her writing have been featured in *Vogue*, *Time*, NPR, *Forbes*, *HuffPost*, *Health*, *Shape*, and more. She lives in the San Francisco Bay Area with her family.